CLASS WORK

by

Peter Rowley

Political upheaval, stunning change, an economy on a roller coaster as seen through the eyes of Grimsby school leavers from the 1970s to the present. Their life experiences share a common thread with so many northern towns coping with the aftershock of de-industrialisation and the loss of a whole way of life.

In their own words they demonstrate the achievements, grit and determination of strong characters overcoming life's setbacks.

All profit accrued from the sale of this book will be divided equally between The Shalom Youth Centre and Your Place Community Church.

I have used the names that the contributors were known by when at school (maiden names) and the addresses are where they lived during that time.

TABLE OF CONTENTS

CLASS WORK

Let's drink to the hardworking people

Let's drink to the lowly of birth

Raise your glass to the good and the evil

Let's drink to the salt of the earth.

"Salt of the Earth" from Beggar's Banquet

The Rolling Stones, 1968

As soon as you're born they make you feel small

By giving you no time instead of it all.

"Working Class Hero"

John Lennon, 1970

Ready to come ashore, wages in my hand

Brand new suit, I guess I've no real plans.

"Three Day Millionaires"

John Wood

PREFACE – THE GREAT DECEPTION
(VAN MORRISON, 1973)

1957 – Rising Sun Colliery, Wallsend

I'm almost nine years of age and I'm filled with a mixture of fear and excitement. But mainly excitement, because I'm in the cage with my Uncle Jack and we're dropping like a stone and going underground. Coal is King. My Uncle Jack is the Engineer at the Rising Sun Colliery and lives opposite the pit in a row of miners' houses. It is a Sunday afternoon. There is no production, just a bit of maintenance and we look around and he shows me the pit ponies and the various coal faces and tunnels.

I grew up in North Shields where the chief industry was building and repairing ships. The bestselling historian Paul Kennedy grew up on Tyneside in the 50s and 60s like me. He described it as "a world of great noise and much dirt". I can remember as a young boy many ships being launched and looking about for people you knew. This was an integrated productive community.

1967 - Smiths Dock Repair Yard, North Shields

Fast forward ten years and I'm working in the Fitting Shop as a Slinger in Smiths – dubbed locally as the biggest ship repair yard in the world. Already the cracks are beginning to show. The vast conglomeration of turners and welders, fitters and overhead cranes resembles something out of the hungry thirties. By any standards

2

most of the machines are industrial antiques. Many tradesmen bring in tools from home to keep the job moving. However, this is a two-way street. The maxim that "It's not what you earn it's what you take home" was applied regularly. Walking around the town, the allotments, pigeon lofts and garden sheds were always painted in battleship grey or the colour of whatever boat was in for a refit.

Walking around the Tyne today, there is no industry to replace the great firms like Swan Hunter and Smiths, there is only acres of muddy wasteland that haven't lured a buyer.

Saturday 14th March 2009 – National Union of Mineworkers' Offices, Barnsley

I am sitting in the great Miners' Hall at Barnsley at the annual David Jones and Joe Green Memorial Lecture. Every year wreaths are laid at the memorial outside the Hall before the annual lecture begins. The Great Hall is covered in ornate miners' banners and the audience of about 500 means standing room only. David Gareth Jones, died amid violent scenes outside Ollerton Colliery in Nottinghamshire on the 15th March 1984. Joe Green was crushed to death by a lorry while picketing in Ferrybridge, West Yorkshire.

I have seen the main speaker, Arthur Scargill on many occasions. That Saturday morning he seemed to fill the stage such was the power of his oratory. He said the two men had paid the "ultimate price" for their cause; "one of the noblest causes this class has ever known".

"David Jones was at the beginning of his life, a young man with everything to look forward to. When I visited his family I did not know what to say. How do you speak to a mother and father whose son has just been killed?"

Over 15,000 Yorkshire Miners and miners from all British coalfields attended the funerals of both men.

The defeat of the 1984 Miners Strike devastated areas like Barnsley. John Redwood, then Thatcher's Policy Chief argued that all the government wanted to do was modernise the industry. But the coal industry was not modernised, or even consolidated, it was decimated, it was murdered.

When the pits shut, a whole way of life disappeared overnight. The massive shock this created meant the entire economic system and social infrastructure supporting mining areas vanished. Thatcher's government simply walked away with no transition plan in place for the people and communities they had destroyed.

Many miners never worked again, some became self-employed or got jobs in the low paying sectors of retail and distribution, usually non-unionised in the new "flexible" economy.

Recovering from Thatcher's legacy remains a huge challenge in areas like Barnsley today. To arrest the structural, long-lasting and inter-generational atrophying of the local economy would require 30,000 new jobs and weekly wages would need to increase by £60 to reach the national average.

Visiting Barnsley, I am constantly reminded of the anger felt, even today by the locals. Most cannot forget and certainly not forgive, what has been inflicted on some of Britain's best communities.

Durham Miners Gala – 8th July 2017

Standing with Babs among 200,000 people on the 133rd Miners Gala – the biggest gathering of trade unionists and left-wing supporters in Europe. Although the last pit closed in Durham years ago the bands and banners are still here, very much alive. Perversely, due to the sterling efforts of the Durham Miners Association, the event goes from strength to strength and this year provided the biggest crowd for decades. The platform speakers and guests include Dennis Skinner, a real Gala favourite, many trade union leaders, the film maker Ken Loach and of course Jeremy Corbyn. The politics are inspirational, but the Gala is also a community event aiming to preserve the values of solidarity and mutual help and support so redolent in the former mining communities. Values that are even more vital than ever in Britain today where decent employment opportunities become scarce, and the State withdraws from the principles of the Welfare State.

Davey Hopper the late Secretary of the Durham Miners made a very prescient speech at the Gala in 2014.

Perhaps anticipating a sea change was in the air, he boomed.

"I firmly believe that if the labour party campaigned with some passion and commitment to reverse these privatisation rip offs, restore the utilities to the people and declare there will be no more cutbacks or privatisation of the NHS, it would stem the flow of disillusioned voters away from its ranks, revive its core and create a tidal wave of support. There are of course, other pressing issues, zero hours contracts, unemployment, homelessness and housing which also requires tackling with the radical spirit that gripped post-war Labour.

"This lack of a radical alternative is turning hundreds of thousands off politics …"

The move by Labour under Jeremy Corbyn to address all of these issues has meant a total change of direction and a reinvigoration of the Left in British politics.

Davey Hopper summed up in his typical uncompromising fashion.

"Our Gala today is as important as ever as a rallying point against injustice and exploitation.

"So let this, the 130th Gala, commemorating the gigantic struggle of 1984/85, put down a new marker to change this rotten capitalist system which has failed the working class so spectacularly."

Only an interventionist government with courage and ability can confront the challenges of the future and the mistakes of the past. Standing aside and allowing the "market" to determine winners and losers has been an absolute disaster for Grimsby, Barnsley, Durham and the former industrial heartlands.

It is significant that Corbyn's social democratic 2017 manifesto, espousing policies already in place in more progressive European countries are branded as "dangerous", Marxist" and "lunacy". That is the level of debate thirty years of neo-liberalism has bequeathed.

The point is what has happened in Grimsby is unfortunately not unique as we have seen. As you move from the North East the pattern is replicated in the North West, the Midlands and even the old industrial parts of suburban London.

The process of deindustrialization has been legitimised by both Tory and Labour governments alike for the past 30 – 40 years. The arguments run as follows. One, the old "smokestack" heavy industries are not the future, the future is the "knowledge economy". Secondly, the job of government is to get out of the way and let the free market run riot. Finally, despite all the evidence to the contrary in almost every facet of national life from

World Cup tournament football to exporting our goods and services, free trade and open markets are required. After all, Britain can always outrun the competition when the chips are down, can't it?

As so very often in contemporary Britain, the image and the rhetoric are a far cry from the reality. What was sold to the public as a new dawn for Britain has led to industrial decay and decimation with far too little replacing it.

There have been three phases in the de-industrialization process. The Thatcher government, the monetarist experiment, and the deregulation of the City of London, ushered in a housing boom, privatisations and a manufacturing sector in free fall. The redundant skilled engineers were not absorbed into the new economy – they were either on the scrapheap or in de-skilled poorly paid employment.

New Labour, Blair, Brown and Mandelson, put a much more optimistic spin on the whole process. Mandelson declared Silicon Valley his "inspiration" and lionised the "knowledge economy". The future lay in importing cheaper manufactured products from abroad while we concentrated on software, the creative sector, financial services, culture and tourism. When Mandelson in his second coming realised how vacuous all this was, he stated "There needs to be far less financial engineering and more real engineering".

It was all looking a little too late. Britain's industrial decline has been the most dramatic in Europe since the war. In 1979, yes as late as this, manufacturing accounted for 30% of Britain's national income and employed nearly seven million. No other economy has experienced this economic shock. The Germans and French have practised industrial husbandry and preserved their big hitters and domestic supply chains. Britain has patently failed to do this and there is plenty of evidence that this is not only bad economics, the effects on society and community cohesion have been disastrous.

The once great powerhouse of steel, coal, shipbuilding and engineering, the North East, is now the call centre capital of Britain.

Osborne has paid lip service to the analysis that Britain's economy is seriously unbalanced. His responses have been facile – "The Northern Powerhouse" – "The Midlands Engine" - empty sloganeering without any patient analysis and implementation of an over-arching industrial strategy.

"Regeneration", is applied to the creation of giant shopping centres, without any apparent irony. What was once a culture of production, of making and selling products, has moved to a consumerist culture of buying things instead, increasingly with credit.

Pundits, journalists and politicians, both locally here in Grimsby and nationally often bemoan the loss of community spirit. They don't seem to factor in the wrecking ball that has been used on these communities.

As one former shipyard worker interviewed on TV stated when asked if he had found employment after redundancy.

"Yes, we're all working – we sell each other sandwiches."

This, in far too many examples, is the reality of the Tory "jobs miracle". The boast of the "strong economy" ignores our total inability to pay our way internationally with record deficits in trade, and productivity inferior to our competitors.

In Grimsby almost seven out of ten voted to leave the EU. Rachel Shabi, the journalist and broadcaster, described this as the day "Fate finally caught up with free market capitalism."

She went on to argue that falling wages, rising costs, work insecurity and the axe taken to the Welfare State had meant anaemic growth and stalling productivity. However, following the crash of 2008, the rising tide of anger had no real outlet in parliament as Labour offered no coherent articulation of the alternatives other than grinding austerity.

She argues that a large chunk of this despair was like a letter delivered to the wrong address, with Brexit the result.

Boris Johnson, the Foreign Secretary, produced a 4,000-word article in the Telegraph blaming almost all of Britain's ills on the meddling of the European super state. After Brexit with one bound we are free. The new alchemy will be tax cuts, cutting red tape and doing incredible trade deals as "Global Britain". This will lead to rising wages and boosted productivity.

At least Johnson acknowledges the undoubted problems in our economy. His analysis of their causes, however is risible.

It was not Brussels' regulations that have produced low wages and the "gig economy". Britain's harsh labour laws and the emasculation of organised labour was enacted by Tories here in Britain.

It was not Brussels that increased desperate poverty and widespread foodbanks. It was Osborne's attack on the social contract which have caused England to have 8 out of 10 of the poorest regions in Northern Europe.

Britain's inability to develop policies that spread income, work and opportunity around the country is well and truly minted at home.

The Thatcherite utopia of sunlit uplands, and life as a buccaneering global trader is unlikely as rhetoric is challenged by reality. The platitudes of gilded Etonians like Johnson and Jacob Rees Mogg, suggest conservative thinking only tenuously in touch with reality.

Britain does need a wholesale refashioning of its economic and social model. However, it is the pursuit of a Thatcherite utopia espoused by Johnson, that is the true cause of our current plight. It offers absolutely no answers to the problems facing towns like Grimsby, Barnsley and Durham, and indeed the wider economy.

INTRODUCTION

Few periods in post war Britain have been as controversial and tumultuous as the years 1970 – 1974 and 1979 – 1986.

Stunning change and economic and social upheaval dominated events as successive administrations attempted to confront the deep-rooted problems facing British Capitalism.

But how did these events effect and resonate on the lives of ordinary people who lived through both periods? I have tried to examine the key policies and events of the time and look at their impact on the transition from school to work.

The evidence is garnered from my experience as a teacher at the Harold Secondary School in Grimsby and latterly as a Lecturer at Grimsby College of Technology where the former school became an annexe.

The school, now demolished, was based at the heart of Grimsby's East Marsh district. In the seventies it was a solid working-class community with strong links to the town's dominant industry – fishing. Now, like many areas where the industry that gave the area its meaning and identity have declined, it faces immense problems.

The experiences and life stories of those interviewed by me reflect achievements, grit and the determination of some very strong characters. They show in so many cases, just what people are capable of when offered an opportunity and reject the notion that if you start disadvantaged you will always struggle.

Viewed from today's standpoint the experiences of school leavers in the seventies and then the eighties are unrecognisable. In the seventies there were plenty of jobs but little training. The quality of many jobs and the lack of any provision of ongoing training or education was a major worry. In the eighties the jobs disappeared to be replaced by "training". The deadest of dead end jobs were presented as the new youth Eldorado and the response to mass unemployment was near-compulsory training and work experience.

In summary two extremes of the spectrum. The seventies, work without training. The eighties, training without work.

Both of these phases saw a Tory government proposing radical solutions to the long-term decline of the economy. Their impact on Grimsby's school leavers was to be profound.

PART ONE 1970 – 1974

"Call out the instigators because there's something in the air. We've got to get together sooner or later because the revolution is here".

Thunderclap Newman, 1970

The clearest rejection of what became known as the post-war consensus was, ironically, given by the Prime Minister James Callaghan at the 1976 Labour Party Conference.

"We used to think you could spend your way out of recession and increase employment by boosting government spending" he boomed.

"I tell you, in all candour, "he went on "that that option no longer exists. In so far as it ever did exist, it only worked on each occasion by injecting a bigger dose of inflation into the economy, followed by a higher level of unemployment as the next step."

It is impossible to write about this period without a short history of the thinking behind this statement. The debate still dominates contemporary politics in Britain today.

Let's de-mystify all the jargon and implicit assumptions within the speech.

Towards the end of the Second World War William Beveridge produced a paper entitled "Social Insurance and Allied Services". This stated, following on from the bitter memories of the 1930's slump, that it was the government's responsibility to deliver "full employment". Let no one be in any doubt just how dramatic a concept this was.

However, aspiring to something is not the same as delivering on a promise. The clear difference between the 1930's and the post-war period was that now governments were confident they had the correct policy response to recessions and downturns endemic in a capitalist economy.

Their confidence was inspired by the work of John Maynard Keynes based on his seminal analysis "The General Theory of Employment Interest and Money".

Like most good ideas, once the penny drops, it all looks so obvious.

Keynes explained that there was a certain level of spending or "demand" needed to buy the goods and services to keep and retain "full employment". He broke spending down into three components; consumer spending (C) - what you or I buy in the course of our weekly outgoings. Investment (I) – what companies spend on capital goods and productive equipment. Finally, Government spending (G) crucial to all areas of the public realm, especially following the creation of the Welfare State.

Keynes constructed a simple formula: -

$$C + I + G = AMD$$

AMD simply stands for Aggregate (or total) Monetary Demand – the total level of spending in an economy.

The trick was to ensure that if unemployment was to rise, one or all of the above would need to be boosted, depending on the depth of the problem.

Thus a government could lower interest rates to boost consumer spending, or give firms major incentives to invest in new equipment. Finally, it could grasp the nettle and boost demand through development of public works and infrastructure programmes.

An early example of this would be Roosevelt's "New Deal" which revitalised the moribund economy of the Tennessee Valley with a massive programme of construction featuring roads and dams.

Keynes also asserted an equally challenging theory – especially in the light of George Osborne's austerity economics. The bombshell was that all this demand injected into the economy to generate full employment would actually pay for itself. How? Because all the extra tax receipts from wage earners and the cutting of benefit payments of all types were just one of the reasons why this was self-financing.

So Keynes' economics were light years away from the corner shop mentality and "common sense" mantras of the devotees of Thatcher. "Living within your means" and "You can't spend what you don't earn" were viewed as nonsense by Keynes if the economy was running at less than full speed. Spending or investment to achieve desired objectives and then achieving payback at the conclusion seemed an eminently more "common sense" approach.

So, "Deficit financing" which Keynes viewed as "self financing" was a direct challenge to austerity and the self-defeating strategies of lowering spending to balance budgets. The lessons of the 1930s were that for all the rigour that cuts were applied the economy flatlined with all the human cost and misery this implied.

Thus Keynesian economics was nothing short of a major rejection of the policies applied inter war and ironically huge elements of "Osborne Economics" today.

The post-war consensus as it became known meant that the two major parties, both Labour and Conservative applied Keynes' ideas to create the conditions for what became known as the "Long Boom" from 1945 to the mid-sixties. This was an absolutely unprecedented period of prolonged full employment and economic expansion and represented a practical vindication of Keynesian ideas.

If, as it undoubtedly was, as successful as its devotees demonstrated, why was it challenged and ultimately rejected? Many of the clues to its demise lay in its brutal rejection as outlined by Callaghan earlier in this chapter.

The "Long Boom" was the high-water mark of consensus politics. This was expressed as a "historic compromise" adopted by both Labour and Conservative governments. The terms of this compromise were capital and big business agreed to the basic reforms enshrined in the Welfare State and promised to provide rising standards of living and full employment. The organised working class confined its demands within narrow political and economic limits, neither seeking too great a share of the national cake, or mounting any serious challenge to the economic order or the Establishment.

By its very nature, the success of this compromise assumes that capital is both willing and able to keep its side of the bargain. When this was no longer the case the results were graphic – social conflict, the breakdown of consensus politics and the end of the "Long Boom".

Why did it all go wrong? The answer to this question is very much coloured by your view of how the British Economy and society operates.

Keynesian demand management operates on injecting demand into a flagging economy to avoid recessions or downturns. The sixty-million-dollar question is just how much demand is necessary?

Inject too little and the problem remains unresolved. More crucially inject too much and you create inflation, simply replacing one problem with another. How does this inflation occur? The best analogy is an auction. At this auction are the sum total of all the goods and services available in our economy, no more, no less. However due to pumping in more spending power we now have available more money chasing the same amount of goods, simply "bidding" up prices.

Now we see the thinking behind Callaghan's speech.

Trying to second guess the timing and behaviour of millions of consumers and interest groups in an economy using demand management was proving ever more difficult. In a mixed economy you can't control what you don't own. Even today with the wealth of data and statistics available to governments just monitor any news broadcast – there is always a "surprising" jump in unemployment or an "unexpected" rise in prices.

Coupled with Keynesianism running out of steam was the even bigger problem of the long term relative decline of the British Economy. Our economy compared to our industrial competitors has been trapped in a vicious cycle of low investment, leading to low pay and productivity and increasing job insecurity.

This was in contrast to the post war economic titans Germany, Japan, France, South Korea and China who were in a virtuous cycle – a long term approach to investment and constant modernisation producing large leaps in productivity and market capture.

Britain's capitalist class took advantage of the "Long Boom" where a post war restocking boom created a tide allowing all boats to rise. Britain's "wealth creators" opted for instant gratification after the Second World War. Post war exports and profits were guaranteed by massive reconstruction projects across Europe and the world even given British capital's singular lack of investment in capital goods and machine tools.

This "investment strike" has resulted in the huge disparities in productivity between Britain and most of the economic "big hitters". The problem is so deep-seated it confounds our present government who seem unable to rectify our loss of markets, industry and high quality well-paid employment.

The UK endures a further handicap in that Finance Capital and the primacy of the City of London has created a seriously unbalanced economy.

In order to maintain sterling as a reserve currency and the City as one of the centres of global finance certain policy priorities are maintained. These are often deemed "Hard Money" policies and demand high interest rates and a strong pound. This may create the ideal conditions for City dealers, but it is the last thing that manufacturers, especially in the export sector, require.

Thus, above and beyond the lack of investment and the death of skills training, Britain's industrial base has had to contend with an over-valued pound and punitive interest rates if they require funds for growth and expansion. Given that the city has deep pockets in terms of its backing for the Tory party and the class background of their MPs industry and manufacturing have for too long been an undervalued afterthought.

This has produced a process dubbed "deindustrialisation". This has been graphically illustrated in the origins of the three bridges across the Forth in Scotland. Two English civil engineers designed the original railway bridge; a Scottish contractor erected it using steelwork from South Wales and Scotland. The 1964 second bridge followed a similar roll-out – British designers and a consortium of construction firms – Cleveland Bridge and Engineering Company, and Dorman Long Limited carried out the work.

Contrast this with the latest bridge over the Forth. There is a tiny British input. A few box girders from Cleveland Bridge, a safety monitoring system from the Arup Group and only 16% of the construction by Morrison Construction.

Today the main designers are represented by America, Germany, Holland, Denmark and Sweden. The steel comes from China; the concrete from Germany and the cable stays from Switzerland.

Thus the end of the "Long Boom" coupled with the increasing vulnerability of adequate policy responses ushered in by 1970 a radical response.

When a compromise, in this case between British Capital and organised Labour begins to fracture an impasse is created. This impasse is eventually resolved by a radical response from one side or the other. The outcome of this response being dependant on the balance of class forces at the time.

This radical response was the election of the Health Government which created an upheaval which still resonates and is relevant today almost fifty years later.

In an early intervention in the subsequent history of "soundbites" Heath promised, in the final days of the 1970 General Election "to cut prices at a stroke". This was thought to do just enough to provide a surprise victory, although no plausible explanation was offered how he proposed to achieve this.

Heath advocated a radical new departure from the failing consensus to really turn Britain around. The TV programme Panorama dubbed him "The man for those Conservatives who think the party needs a tiger in its tank".

In January 1970 following a cabinet strategy meeting at the Selsdon Park Hotel, Heath reportedly fleshed out his new approach. With tax cuts and a rolling back of the State, he also proposed setting industry free to stand on its own two feet, where winners would flourish and expand and losers would be shaken out. "Lame Ducks" – a phrase which subsequently haunted the administration were not to be assisted.

In his avowal of market forces, the stiff wind of competition, and a reduced role for the State Heath aimed to break with the fraying consensus and revitalise and re-energise the nation. Concurrently in order to minimise working class resistance, industrial relations adopted a more coercive and administrative approach as exemplified by the Industrial Relations Act.

In hindsight, Heath adopted a "pre-Thatcherite" position in the initial phase of his stewardship.

However, the more aggressive approach to industrial relations led to trade union militancy unparalleled since the 1920's. The result of the Industrial Relations Act saw Britain on the brink of its first General Strike since 1926 following the imprisonment of the dockworkers – "The Pentonville 5" – subsequently released by mass extra-parliamentary action.

Other notable acts of defiance were the UCS work-in where Clydside workers refused to accept planned closures and took over their yards.

Jimmy Reid, one of the architects of the "work in", became an overnight sensation. Adept as using the media, and with a formidable grasp of economics and politics he ran rings around the Government spokesmen. Telling phrases such as "Their approach is not just pre-Keynesian it is prehistoric". He labelled Government ministers "Hard faced political gangsters". His charisma, coupled with the disciplined and dignified conduct of the occupation meant the Government failed in the propaganda war and eventually withdrew closure plans. Two miners' strikes against incomes policies saw further humiliations, lights out, 3-day weeks and States of Emergency declared. In a final throw of the dice Heath attempted to win a "one issue election". "Who runs the country? The elected government or the Trade Union militants?" However, such was the antipathy aroused by the Tories, Heath got the wrong, albeit graphic answer, "Not you chum". He lost the election and

Wilson returned to power promising to heal the country, calm down industrial relations, and restore harmony.

Heath's term in office 1970 – 1974 produced turmoil and unrest on an unprecedented scale. His attempt to break, at least initially, with the post-war consensus was a radical admission that it was failing to deliver. His planned departure from consensus politics collapsed because he failed to take account of the terrain in which he was operating. A strong, confident and unionised working class were not prepared to accept the dismantling of the support mechanisms of the Welfare State. They challenged Heath at every juncture and this stiff rather solitary man never really managed to take public opinion with him.

Perhaps the other major oversight was that too many of his party, those Thatcher would later dub the "Wets" were reluctant to take the required hard determined approach. "One Nation" Tories steeped in the philosophies of Macmillan saw Heath's approach as a "bridge too far".

Thus Heath moved from a pre-Thatcherite position in the face of huge opposition, to a more orthodox corporate mode of intervention and pragmatism. However, by then his decline was inevitable and his position irreversible. His failure stemmed from a working class with the power and organisation to fight the ending of the post-war settlement, and a Tory Party lacking the will to give it their unqualified backing.

Now let's fast forward to Britain today in 2017. A Britain riven with division and the populism that is the direct result of four decades of economic failure. The failures since the financial crisis and before have created Brexit in Britain and Trump in America. The doctrines of the last forty years are often termed neo-liberalism.

What are the main features of this doctrine? Basically that the public sector is a burden and a burden that must be systematically reduced and replaced with the dynamism of the private sector. Keynesianism and economic management were to be abandoned in favour of a market-orientated approach where governments shunned intervention. There was a brutal assertion of "management's right to manage" and trade unions, seen as an impediment to efficient labour markets, were to be emasculated.

Tax incentives were given to the "wealth creators" in order to turbo charge the economy. However, it was decreed that rather than a small coterie of "winners" everyone would benefit from wealth cascading down to the remainder under the "trickledown effect". Initially the two major exponents of neo-liberalism, which shall be examined more fully later were Thatcher here, and Reagan in the USA.

It has become increasingly clear that rather than "an economy which works for everyone not just the few" these policies have produced the complete opposite effect.

The division of the economic spoils both here and in America have followed an identical pattern, with the lion's share going to the minority.

Contrast the following statistics. When the US was doing well, between 1961 and 1969 the bottom 90% of Americans took 67% of the income gains. During the boom years prior to the financial crash between 2001 to 2007 they got just 2% of the extra income generated while the 10% took a gargantuan 90%.

Austerity economics in the UK have neither restored the public finances denuded from the crash, or halted the decline in real wages. The drive for more and more labour market flexibility has produced the advent of the "Gig Economy" zero hours contracts and bogus self-employment. Productivity lags far behind our competitors as employers have substituted cheap labour for capital investment. The failure of real wages to maintain their purchasing power have created debt-fuelled bubbles that like all bubbles eventually burst to tip the economy back into recession.

Increasing cynicism and detachment from the electorate and inadequate policy responses from governments point to a massive problem for exponents of the current system. When the next crisis arrives will they advocate more of the same and will people continue to swallow economic medicine which patently does not offer a cure?

The idea of Britain emerging as a great global trader following Brexit looks to be pure fantasy. Currently, even with the collapse of sterling which should make our exports more attractive, this is not happening. In fact the Balance of Payments deficit is worse than ever. Before Britain embarks on a trade strategy it requires a coherent Industrial Strategy to ensure we can produce the goods and services the rest of the world demand. This is not happening and without it a return to well-paid meaningful work looks to be a triumph of wishful thinking over reality. Britain's Brexit strategy has been described as a wish list, or more cruelly "A letter to Santa Clause".

"Thatcherism" as it came to be dubbed therefore confronted and largely overcame the obstacles that stopped Heath in his tracks. In terms of the environment for school leavers in the two periods we examine the 1970 – 74 phase looks extremely benign compared to the deal offered to school leavers in the eighties in what became dubbed the "Great Training Robbery".

The cohesiveness and community spirit of the East marsh was to be tested to breaking point over the period. Working class solidarity based on shared experience and support was an anathema to a philosophy emphasising the aggressive individualism and "no such thing as society" espoused by Thatcherism.

SCHOOL LEAVERS ON THE EAST MARSH 1969 – 1976

By a quirk of fate, my involvement with the Harold Secondary School in Grimsby's East Marsh was replicated three times in my working life.

In 1969 while at student at Hull College of Education I had to grind through 13 weeks of teaching practice in the winter of 1969. This entailed stopping in digs in the nearby resort of Cleethorpes and returning on the ferry across the Humber to Hull at weekends. Those times pre-dated the construction of the Humber Bridge.

After returning for my final year at college I was unsure what to do next. I was labouring at a sectional building firm in Hull with a good set of lads. I was playing rugby for a cracking side in Hull and was fairly settled. Out of the blue in a life changing moment, Mike Peacock my mentor at Harold Street informed the college of a current vacancy at the school. My interest was immediately reawakened, I applied and started in September 1971. A decision I never regretted.

I was born in North Shields, a town dominated by shipbuilding and repair, fishing and heavy engineering and inevitably in that part of the world coal mining. Indeed, the borough coat of arms for North Shields shows a miner and a fisherman and the inscription "We reap our harvest from the deep". So I didn't experience too much of a culture shock. What was surprising were the wages, less than two thirds of what I had been earning as a labourer in Hull.

Due to the difficulty in attracting teachers Grimsby ran a "key worker" scheme whereby you were guaranteed council accommodation for six months, or in extenuating circumstances up to a year.

I secured a flat on the ninth floor of Garibaldi House. This was next to Grimsby's iconic road, Freeman Street, the "fishermen's street" and had a fantastic view as far up the coast as Cleethorpes and over to the Hull skyline on the north bank.

At this time, well before the "Cod Wars" which marked the terminal decline of the industry, fishing was king. Hundreds of fishermen supported an onshore economy of filleters and processors, transport, docking, taxis, pubs, clubs and small and large businesses.

The "three day millionaires" refers to the free-spending fishermen home to enjoy themselves for the short time they were given before returning to sea.

Freeman Street then was a vital area, full of life, more akin to a wild west frontier town. The massive contrast to the present day is graphic. I recall the lyrics of Bruce Springsteen's "My Home Town" of factory closures, boarded up shops, and people hanging about, inactive and defeated.

Return again to the early seventies, fishermen out and about, identified by their suits, powder blue, bottle green, red, yellow, expensive and distinctive with pleats and belted jackets. A suit for lunchtime and another at night, and taxis their chosen mode of carriage.

The market, packed with shoppers, tailors, jewellers, a plethora of watering holes and a massive conveyor belt of semi-skilled and unskilled employment. A hardworking town, rough and ready, filled with characters who if they were out, were out to enjoy themselves.

With only a ten-minute walk to work, with staff and later pupils who became lifelong friends, I embarked on the most enjoyable and satisfying period of my working life.

"Harold Street" as it was known had served generations of the local community, with hundreds drawn from a tightly knit geographical area. On a crude measurement probably 90% were drawn from within a radius of a half mile of the school.

This bred a sense of community and shared experiences. Generous, loyal and tough, witness their sporting prowess in football and rugby, punching well above their weight against neighbouring giant comprehensives.

Perhaps a recent recollection by an ex-pupil John Taylor on the Harold Street Grimsby Friends Facebook site best sums things up.

"I was visiting Toll Bar School to deliver a careers talk when I bumped into Mr Robinson (my former English teacher and Form Tutor at Harold Street).

Like you do, I asked how stuff was at a very large comprehensive compared to Harold Street and did he like it?

His words paraphrased …

"it's like this …. The kids here think they are better than they are, whereas the kids at Harold Street were better than they were led to believe they were".

Over forty years have passed since those days in the early seventies. It has been a great experience for me revisiting those years and how people have turned out and how they have lived their lives. The changes in their community have been profound and not always for the better. Nevertheless, there is a great deal that is inspirational and demonstrates the resilience and determination required to overcome life's setbacks. This is their story.

"THE HEART OF THE EAST MARSH" - JOHN ELLIS

John Ellis has been a vicar on the East marsh since 1972. He was born in Dun Laogharie, south of Dublin. After three years in Belfast followed by three years in London he came to Grimsby to be part of a three-strong team at the church with a remit to engage with the youth of the area and establish a Youth Club.

The Shalom Youth Club attached to the Church has served hundreds of children in the area. Undoubtedly John and his team have been a massive and positive influence on so many people. In his own words he defines youth work as "Workers and young people build a relationship of mutual trust and respect which enables young people to negotiate the turbulent waters of adolescence and emerge as reasonably functioning adults".

The magnificent personal testimonials from current and ex-members are evidence of the impact John and his team have made on so many people's lives.

I asked John to give his impression of the East Marsh when he arrived in the early seventies.

"Fishing was still ticking over and had a huge cultural impact on the community. There was not a great deal of money about and kids dressed in gear that they wouldn't be seen dead in today. Basically the lads dressed like their fathers in denims and working gear. The area was dominated by two street gangs – The Ice House Gang and the Park Street Mafia. Basically any youth provision needed at least initially to blend into the reality of the territorial nature of gang members. However there was no drug culture to speak of."

I probed a little deeper and asked John what he thought of the children in the area.

"They took some working with. They were tough, tougher than kids now. Their attitudes were forged in the male-orientated and macho fishing culture. There was plenty of work, much of it semi and unskilled work and unlimited opportunities for casual and black-market activities.

"Today, although the area is one of the most deprived in the UK, kids are indulged in terms of clothes, trainers, phones and computers".

John then took me through the history and development of the Shalom and the Church.

"When I arrived in Grimsby I was looking for a change and a new challenge. Initially we opened a club one night per week in the old St John's Church Hall which catered almost exclusively for the Park Street lot.

"Slowly we expanded and were given money from Grimsby Council in 1979 to extend the premises at our current base. Our staff comprised one paid Youth Worker plus eight volunteers, some of whom were members of my congregation."

Although he is ostensibly retired, John still puts in the hours. His Church provides a daily soup kitchen providing hot meals on a daily basis completely free of charge and staffed by a dedicated team of volunteers.

"I was looking through some of the old Church records recently. In 1881 there was a soup kitchen on this site. It records an oxen head being used as stew for the neighbourhood poor. It's like back to the future."

John describes himself today as a political animal.

"Thatcher politicised me. She destroyed this community. People didn't struggle to pay bills like today. I loathe everything she stands for.

"Blair repaired some of the damage. A brand new Sure Start Children's Centre was built in the area, Havelock School was extended and updated and Orchard Drive replaced some of the worst housing."

Of the current Tory administration, he is absolutely scathing.

"They are even worse than Thatcher. The Bedroom Tax and Benefit sanctions mean I deal with people who have had no money for ten weeks. A parishioner looks after her four grandchildren after her daughter died of a drug overdose. She was recently told to find a full time forty-hour week job. It's absolutely outrageous."

I asked John to summarise what he considered his biggest achievements in his long and indeed ongoing career.

"When the old Church collapsed we built a new one on the site. We currently provide for four hundred youngsters a year. Initially our membership was drawn almost exclusively from Harold Street School but now as youth provision elsewhere has been withdrawn our catchment area has expanded."

Today John has hopes for a new scheme to develop social housing and generally revitalise and inject some hope and momentum to an area that has taken some very hard knocks.

"Drugs are an absolute nightmare. Easy money can be made running drugs for dealers among the youth. Worklessness is a major issue. Some struggle badly but in their early twenties many turn things around. Many work away, out of Grimsby in marine support and heavy-duty construction, scaffolding in London and other major cities. Women in general find it slightly easier with some local opportunities in factory work and the Care Sector.

"The area has basically slid off a cliff. Drugs are endemic. However a strong community has managed to hold itself together in spite of everything. It is a waste of so many lives and so much potential."

Almost as an afterthought I asked John to comment on "Skint" the TV programme which centred on Grimsby and the East Marsh's problems. John's was one of the very few organisations who took part in the programme. Many boycotted any involvement on the grounds that anything positive would end up on the cutting room floor as programmes searched for sensationalised "poverty porn" viewing.

John said "I have nothing but praise for the programme makers. They were very fair and if more had participated we might have had a more balanced coverage throughout the series. We received a flood of donations from viewers throughout the UK when the programme ended".

John has been and continues to be a towering figure in the area. His biggest achievement is one he is too modest to mention, the huge and positive impact he has had on so many lives in the East Marsh.

"LONG PROMISED ROAD" – BEVERLY LINES
(THE BEACH BOYS, 1971)

79 CASTLE STREET, 1972 – 1977

In 1964 a ground-breaking TV documentary "Seven UP" followed the lives of children from widely different backgrounds about their lives, their ambitions and their opinions. It was to have a massive impact, and in fact they returned every seven years to track how their individual stories unfolded.

What was striking to me was the absolute confidence with which middle class children viewed their world. One sticks in my mind today, he currently attended a pre-Prep school in Kensington and then mapped out a career path which entailed public school and even the exact Cambridge College he would attend before going on to a career in the law. All this he subsequently achieved.

The same surety and over-confidence in their ability is displayed graphically by three politicians, David Cameron, Boris Johnson and

41

George Osborne. The left-wing MP Dennis Skinner often jibes that such people "Have been educated beyond their ability". Given the mess which all three have made in my opinion, it is difficult to argue with this view. The whole array of contacts and advantages enjoyed by this privileged elite endows a total self-belief often belying their incompetence and lack of judgement.

The corollary of this of course is that many very intelligent and able working class school leavers lack the confidence and the advice to enable them to fulfil their potential.

I interviewed Beverley at her home and started out by asking her about her upbringing.

"I was one of nine. We never seemed to be bored. I was very well looked after and there was always good food on the table. I spent a lot of time at my Dad's allotment and at Graham Stiffel's listening to music – Queen, Supertramp, Cockney Rebel, Black Sabbath. My elder brother was in the Royal navy and always brought things home on shore leave – a shoebox cassette player, guitar and bongo drums. We were very family centred, although I smoked my first cigarette at eleven and we used to drink cider down the back alley.

"I thought Harold Street was a really good school. I really enjoyed it. I loved English with Mrs Blades who taught me for three years. My other favourite was Biology. I didn't enjoy Maths and Mr

Seedall threw me out because I covered my exercise book the wrong way.

"I saw my future in office work and achieved a Grade 1 in typing. I also did further qualifications at night school. This enabled me to get a job at Norris tyres and Norris the Rubberman in the Accounts and Purchase Ledger Department. After two years, I changed to John Sutcliffe Freight Forwarders on Freeman Street. Initially I was in the computer room before moving into Sales Ledger and finally Audit Control

"I had my son Ashley and two years later my daughter Natalie and like most people in those days stayed at home to look after them.

"By then we had moved from Stanley Street to a bigger house on Queen Mary Avenue. I was desperate for a new hall stairs and landing carpet so I started on the 6pm – 10pm shift at Birds Eye. We picked peas on the line and I hated it. Eventually we were made redundant, some were in tears but all I felt was elation. Still, I got that carpet.

"I then took an entirely different route, party planning selling clothes and subsequently bone china from Stoke. I made some decent money at times.

"I wanted to take the kids to Florida so once again I gave Birds Eye a go. The firm established the Springboard Learning Centre to enable the entire workforce to develop themselves. I had always updated myself educationally and my husband John ran a kids' football team for Birds Eye. This demonstrated community activism and I was made a Champion Learner Representative. The GMB union established the centre. I did twenty hours in the factory and sixteen in the Learning Centre. We covered all shifts and also weekends – nobody missed out. Obviously my office skills were very useful and I remained there for 12 years. The centre remained open for three years following the factory closure.

"One of my friends told me about a charity called Foresight that had an opening. I started in administration work then progressed to managing a volunteering service for befriending older people. I started doing awareness training around visual impairment and decided to get myself qualified and after courses at Grimsby college achieved my Certificate in Education at Huddersfield. I then started on a very enjoyable chapter of my working life teaching Health and Social Care students at the College and at Franklin Sixth Form College. After being promoted to Centre Manager at Foresight I decided it was time to move on.

"By now I had both experience and qualifications so in 2010 I got a job at Kensington Care Home in Immingham. I saw an advert for a Deputy Manager at Anchorage, another care home and after a short stint as Deputy was appointed Manager. I have been in the job for over six years and currently we have 36 residents.

Right at the end of our conversation, Beverley said to me.

"I always wanted to make something of myself and I wonder if it would have been different if I had come from a different background and another school. I didn't do a degree until I was over forty."

The answer of course is not so much that it would have been different, it would all have been so much easier.

"HOME IS WHERE THE HEART IS" - IAN SHAWLER
(ELVIS PRESLEY, 1962)

80 PARK STREET, 1973 – 1976

It was fantastic back then. Everyone was your "uncle" or your "aunty". All my friends lived in Hildyard Street and Rutland Street, all really close at hand. Coming home from school I remember women in headscarves sweeping the path, scrubbing the step or simply having a fag and a gossip with friends and neighbours. If your Mum was out, you were always welcomed into neighbours' houses. There was nothing to fear. We used to roam about collecting empty bottles to take back to the pop factory in Hamilton Street. I would sum it up as a time of innocence and trust.

I got a great deal out of school. We moved to Park Street on my birthday in 1973. I went straight into the second year in 2A1. I thoroughly enjoyed it. Although the school was mixed there were separate playgrounds. The usual pastimes were football, British

Bulldog and heading tennis balls up the sloping roofs surrounding the yard.

I enjoyed most lessons, Maths with Mr Seedall, Biology Science and English. I loved swimming and cross country, it was only in the RAF that my interest in football and rugby developed.

My first job, like so many from Harold Street, was at sea, with John Sleight. I was what is known as a "deckie learner" on seine netters. These were smaller boats with a crew of four plus the skipper. Typically we would be out for 10 – 14 days. After the first week of constant sickness I settled and remained with the firm for eight months.

I fancied a move to "big boats" the deep-sea trawlers. I got a job with British United Trawlers (BUT). However there were no current vacancies for Deckie learners, but they said I could be the galley boy and move up to Deckie learner when a position became available.

I would describe my introduction to the galley as a very steep learning curve. Most of it was basic prep work – potatoes and vegetables for the ship's cook. Gradually I picked more and more up, baking bread rolls and graduating to more interesting and complex work. The crew had huge appetites, they worked 18 hours on and 6 off. This meant that food was virtually permanently on the go. Their basic favourites were roast dinners – huge pieces of beef, pork and lamb. The tricky part with every meal was keeping it on the plate, with the constant rolling of the ship. Once we hit the fishing grounds we had fish straight off the deck in every guise possible. Morning fish sandwiches were a special favourite and the cook's signature was Fish Portuguese – a baked fish in a tomato sauce. We only resumed living on rations on the way back once we were steaming home. The work was incredibly hard and the three days in port were for me a time of recuperation. I never really got into the "three-day millionaire" scenario. We fished Bear island, the White Sea, the Faroes and Iceland.

However, the writing was well and truly on the wall for the industry. My grandfather was a trawler engineer and my stepfather was a "lumper". My mother was concerned and both advised me that a long-term career in fishing was probably no longer achievable.

I decided to leave rather than be pushed or simply drift out of the industry. In a complete change of direction, I got a job in Presto's warehouse in the Bullring. I worked with an older guy called Pete who was ex-military. One day we were having a pint in the Pestle and Mortar and I recognised an old mate called Dave Waters. When I asked what he was up to he said, "I'm in the RAF and it is the best thing I've ever done".

This had a big impact on me and I began mulling things over. A workmate bet me I wouldn't do anything but within a fortnight I had made a life-changing decision. I went down to the Careers

Information Office on Freeman Street and took the aptitude test. I've always been colour blind and so my choice of career options condensed accordingly. I thought I always enjoyed Science and Biology and so chose to be an RAF Medic.

I was in the RAF from the 12th August 1980 to the 1st July 2014 – almost 34 years.

Looking back it was a career of extremes, I enjoyed some fantastic times and some horrible times. I have seen the very best and the worst in people.

I have been in operational and conflict zones in the Falklands, the Gulf War, Saudia Arabia, Iraq and Afghanistan.

I have also been on tours to Australia, Hong Kong, Cyprus, Central and North America, Canada and was also stationed in Germany for three years.

By the end of my service I had attained the rank of Warrant Officer responsible for all non-commissioned officers, managing policy and acting as a focal point for the RAF Medical Services worldwide.

I decided to retire in 2014. My wife had a job at Lincoln and it seemed an obvious fit. I never considered moving elsewhere. My roots are here and I love the place.

I had no job but was contacted by some old friends to go to Sierra Leone during the Ebola crisis. I then did some work for the MOD as a practice Manager in London. I moved on to be Business Manager for a large medical centre in Bridlington.

I decided this wasn't what I wanted and got a job at CK Services Plastics Recycling as a Team Leader. Ironically it was based on the old RAF Binbrook site where I started my service career. Unfortunately the company went into liquidation in 2016. My former manager contacted me and I started with him at a firm called Plasgram at March in Cambridgeshire. Once again they ran into difficulties and redundancies were in the offing. I came home and did agency work lorry driving and fork lift truck work.

I am currently employed by Partners in Hygiene as Night Hygiene Manager. Although initially new to the job, I was employed for my management experience and ability to motivate and communicate with people. I have a Masters Degree in Leadership and Management but I have some basic rules which have always stood me in good stead. I manage as I would wish to be managed and I believe in communicating and giving feedback. I find that I have a very committed workforce who achieve good results and I believe in thanking them for their positive performance.

Although there was a slump following the aftershock of fishing's decline and work was difficult to come by, I believe renewables could point to a brighter future. Dong Energy and Siemens are bit hitters and are now located in Grimsby.

I love Grimsby, I was born here and I'm proud to be a Grimberian. When I hear people knocking it I think I've been to Kabul and Basra – everywhere has its downside. You can't be forever looking back, change is inevitable, you need to live for today and get on with life.

"A SALTY DOG" – JEFF REEDER
(PROCUL HAREM, 1968)

53 HAROLD STREET, 1969 – 1974

"I only remember it as a fantastic time to grow up. Nobody locked doors. When my Dad came home from sea, all the neighbours got fish. It was the same when their Dads docked, there was a culture of sharing and supporting each other. The winters were hard then, playing out we had socks on our hands, we didn't have the luxury of gloves. We played out and roamed all over although Grant Thorold and Sidney park were our favourite football venues. My big mates were Pete Tasker, Les Allen, Alan Redgrift and Rob Rowntree. After school our favourite pastime was drinking cans of beer stolen from Rob's brothers when they came in from sea. We used to have a drink and smoke in his garden shed. After tea it was time for a bit of foraging to get some cash in. Me and Pete Tasker used to strip copper and lead from the houses up for clearance. Sometimes getting the big prize – a copper boiler. Fridays we weighed in our scrap at Jonathan Potts on King Edward Street usually getting £15 to £20 and occasionally £30 – a big deal in those days.

My Mam died when I was five. My Dad was at sea and he was flown in from Iceland at the time. Basically I was brought up by my eldest sister who was twelve and a lady who lived four doors away. She was a widow whose husband was killed in the war. She was a good woman who brought me up until I left Harold Street.

I then moved in with Les Allen's Mam in Phelps Street and went with them when they moved to Harrington Street.

In an illustration of what a small world it is, Jeff told me that their next-door neighbour was John Ellis, the founder of Shalom Youth Club.

My first job was at Lion Fisheries down Orwell Street. I got the job through my sister who worked there. Basically I was labouring, "heavy gang" work as it was known locally. After two months I went down dock, took the medical and got my Port Record Book. I had two trips with consuls Fisheries on the Gillingham. This was followed by a year on the Blackburn Rovers. The Cod War was the last nail in the coffin of Grimsby's Deep Water fleet. My old mate Les Allen was seine netting at the time and he said I would be better off coming with them if I wanted to stay in the industry.

So I went as a trainee – basically a dogsbody making breakfasts, gutting fish, chopping ice. We grafted, in summer we started at 4 a.m. and finished 18 hours later at 10 p.m. In winter it was 6 a.m. until 7 – 8 p.m. – you can't really fish in the dark. Fishing is the hardest of jobs. You have to condition yourself to take the rough with the smooth. I've been on trips where the sea was like a millpond and then where we have been in force seven gales. I've been at sea in two hurricanes and I don't mind admitting I was scared to death, for twenty-four hours we were in the eye of the storm.

When I look back I have no regrets. I then went seine netting for fifteen years then Gill netting for two years in the English Channel. We fished for cod and pollock. After September we used to go long lining off Lowestoft for cod, whiting and skate. We slept in the boat at Lowestoft and came home in the skipper's car typically once a fortnight.

Beam trawling should be banned, it totally destroys the marine ecology. I think fish stocks have held up well in the North Sea otherwise.

I left fishing in 1992 primarily because my daughter was very ill. I'd had a good run and fished longer than most in Grimsby. Things in the industry were in a tailspin of decline. The owners were decommissioning boats to secure big government payouts. As usual it was the workers who got nothing. There was no redundancy scheme and no union, we were classed as casual labour.

Coming ashore I wondered what I would do. I had learned the practicalities of painting and decorating at Glen Parva Borstal in Leicester. I decided to put it to good use. I had three years at it before I became a full-time carer for my daughter. She is now fixed up in independent living accommodation.

Lately things have been looking up for me. Sometimes life looks kindly on you. In the seventies I met a lad from Hartlepool called Major Hartley. Because he was far from home I looked after him, with the odd pint and meal. I even sailed with him a few times but he returned to Hartlepool and we lost touch.

By a complete quirk of fate he docked in Grimsby and we bumped into each other on Freeman Street. He was by now a very wealthy man owning a number of boats. We swapped numbers and kept in touch.

He rang me up and said I've got a job for you. The ship, the Scanboy is used to guard marine pipelines and divert shipping. I do all the cooking for the crew and the cabin and facilities are unbelievable. I specialise in roast dinners, fish and fish cakes and will make more exotic meals although I'm not particularly partial myself.

The prospects and pay look good and he is looking to bring a boat down to Grimsby to enable me to sail from my home port.

Obviously I'm back living on the East Marsh here on Weelsby Street. As I'm in a fisherman's house all my neighbours have connections with the industry. The neighbours are great.

At this point Jeff took me round to his back garden to reveal a communal garden to be shared by all the residents.

"We pay £4 a month for its upkeep and it's a real asset and place to socialise. Having said that I'm not too happy with what goes on in far too many streets round here. Crime and drugs are rife and there is a culture among some Eastern Europeans of hanging about drinking at all hours. I love Freeman Street and enjoy a drink with my mates when onshore.

"BEAR ISLAND AND THE WHITE SEA – NO ELEVEN PLUS FOR ME" - TONY McLERNON

396 CLEETHORPE ROAD, 1969 – 1974

Tony McLernon is a very important figure in this story. First as a pupil at Harold Street and in the second chapter a very good colleague and friend working with me very closely at the Harold Street site running the Youth Training Scheme.

Growing up on the East Marsh, Tony describes a world of monochrome, like an ancient newsreel of social history.

"I loved it. My Dad was an Irish builder and we lived in a big terrace with five bedrooms and a bathroom. We were surrounded by two up and two downs where all my friends lived. Nearly everyone was involved in the fish trade. Major clearance programmes were underway, and they provided endless opportunities for roaming all over derelict sites.

"I was not so politically aware then, but I can remember my Mam cooking on the fire as the Miners' Strikes in the early seventies began to bite and power cuts were invoked.

"We were real foragers and looking back quite entrepreneurial. We emptied bins while the dustmen were on strike. We used to wait at the top of Humber Street for the fishermen who had arrived in dock. We used to carry their kit bags in return for money or sweets while they went to the Humber Pub. To cater for the "three-day millionaires" we used to jump in taxis from the rank at the Clee Park pub and pick up fishermen from Thorold Street.

"Great memories, but higher education or going to University was never on the agenda. In fact when I was supposed to be sitting the eleven plus examination I was absent from school."

Tony went on to explain that throughout his school career he frequently went on what were called, misleadingly in my opinion, "pleasure trips". Going to sea and being part of the crew for the trip.

"I went fishing off Bear Island, the White Sea, Iceland, the Norway coast and the Faroes. I also used to do trips on the inshore boats at weekends."

"The slum clearance programme in the New Clee area where I was brought up meant great upheaval. Street gangs dominated areas and even within the East Marsh it was very territorial.

"Everyone worked, virtually without exception. There was no benefit culture.

"I wanted to be a marine biologist but a lack of parental aspirations and with no clear help or advice on how to progress this ambition, this was never realised.

"On leaving school my first job was as a painter and signwriter at Bemroses. We used to do a great deal of work on the trawlers owned by Consoles. I became restless, especially after the Foreman told me "Don't hang about on this job son, it won't last".

"The death throes of the Grimsby Deep Water Fleet were clearly evident. The oil price shock, the withdrawal of fishing grounds and the politics and decommissioning of ships all pointed to the end of fishing's viability, and to an entire way of life.

"I opted for the building trade and in 1975 I was apprenticed to Tom Wilkinson and Son as a bricklayer. My memories of the national scene at this time were rampant inflation, money didn't stretch; the Cod War with Iceland – a virtual hammer blow to hasten the industry's demise.

"Locally, Barnsley Week at the Fitties provided endless amusement and opportunities. They were turbulent times but there was still plenty of work about.

"I was getting stuck in at work and also doing day release and night school at college. I was good at what I did and I was top apprentice at College three years on the trot, representing the college at national competitions. This led to me being asked to cover a class and some part-time work in the college's building department. I did my Advanced Craft Certificate and did more teaching. The money was good and I enjoyed it.

"The building trade is like a bell-weather for the economy. We generally are first into any recession. The Winter of Discontent was a double whammy for me. Training fell off a cliff and construction work dried up.

"Together with my old Harold Street mates Frank McDonald and Martin Burke we did the "Auf Wiedersehn" bit. For two years we worked all over – Munster, Nordhorn, Hanover, Dortmund and Dusseldorf.

"As I wanted to come back, I managed to get two days' work at the college which quickly became a full-time job with the introduction and rapid expansion of the Youth Training Scheme at the Harold Street Annexe.

"After four good years I landed a job in Cornwall. I was based in Newquay running a training scheme specialising in cottage industries like making surf boards and glass blowing.

"I then took up a post at Kendall college and was based at Morecambe for two years.

"I still hankered for a return to my old stomping ground and after being in some of the most beautiful parts of the UK, returned to Grimsby in 1988. I was now married and self-employed. There was little work locally and the German option was no longer feasible after the turmoil following the fall of the Berlin Wall.

"I landed a job building a reservoir at Covenham and the Clerk of Works suggested I might apply for a job with the Anglian Water Board. The interview was very practical, I was taken round the site and asked to identify any potential snags and problems. I reeled off a number of issues I had spotted and was offered the job on the spot.

"After working locally I was asked to take up the post of Senior Resident Engineer at a Sewage Treatment Plant in New Zealand. Six months lead to an extension of three years with the family joining me. I then took up a post in Dublin Dunleary and Wicklow Bay on a major construction project. It was a great job, I had eighty gangs of contractors working under me and had to deal with all outside agencies including the police and fire service.

"I fancied at job at home and took voluntary redundancy at the end of the contract. After some local building work I returned to Grimsby College in the Construction Department. I then took up a post at a local training provider as head of Assessment and Verification before taking up my present post with North East Lincolnshire Council's training provision.

"As I look at Grimsby today it is hard not to be negative. School leavers who progress to University rarely return and this represents a real brain drain for the area. There may be opportunities in Wind Technology but not in the numbers bandied about in the local press.

"Grimsby has never really recovered from fishing's collapse and there hasn't really been a high technology industry come to Grimsby in the last forty years. There are substantial numbers of young people who have gravitated to areas like Leeds and Manchester. The labour-intensive industries have gone but in my opinion we are still turning out school leavers who can't do much else.

"In my day there was a very strong work ethic and plenty of opportunities. Today the disappearance of those opportunities has inevitably lead to a decline in the work ethic.

"I live in Cleethorpes and have always been a keen sea angler."

Tony does himself down here as he is the author of two books on sea angling which have achieved substantial sales. He is also prolific in competitions, both local and national.

"PADDY HOW DID IT COME TO THIS?" - PADDY JOHNSON
MANGEL STREET, 1971 – 1976

The concept of a job for life takes a battering in most of these personal testimonials. It reflects the reality of both a changing economy and all too often industries in decline unable to withstand the harsh realities of market forces, and the instability caused by frequent recessions and downturns. Paddy's story is no exception.

"I had a good upbringing. My Mam was a strong woman who always stuck up for us. My Dad was a fisherman who died when I was eight years old. He was caught in a winch on deck and died three years later. I arrived home to find my Mam crying over the dolly tub in the yard. She said "Your Dad is dead". Our Roly (brother) had to go to Harold Street to tell the rest of the family.

"I found school very difficult, especially reading – I made virtually no progress while at school. Later in life, I educated myself reading newspapers and got myself up to speed. I loved all sport especially football. I was centre-half in a very good school team and I enjoyed the success and camaraderie.

"When I arrived at Harold Street I was in trouble early on. In morning assembly the teacher playing the piano got more and more animated and we reckoned she was just like the rock and roller Jerry Lee Lewis. Obviously we were giggling and laughing and were hauled out for retribution. Remember this was the early seventies and discipline was ultra strict. The other two received the cane and that was what I expected from Clem Farrel my housemaster. He completely disarmed me in a chat I can remember over 40 years after. He told me that he had heard great things about me from junior school and was convinced this was a one-off and I would soon be back on the straight and narrow. He was a wily old bird and looking back this was probably all nonsense, but nevertheless it worked and had a profound effect on me.

"I was set to follow my Dad and go to sea and even had my medical. However with the closure of the Nautical School you didn't have to be Einstein to see which way the wind was blowing. A family friend told me there was a job as a barrow boy on the fish dock. I got my whites on and was straight into it, delivering up to seventy kit of fish for the filleters, making tea and running errands for their fags and newspapers. On a Friday, pay day they all used to treat me from their own wage packets. They may be rough and ready but they are generous to a fault. My boss was Robbie Blair who stood in Grimsby's election to become an MP. Naturally he was a conservative. I was one of the workforce interviewed by local TV and said I was voting Labour and so were the whole family!

"I started industrial painting and had four years on site at the Redcar Steelworks with a gang all from Harold Street. Today this giant site is mothballed and stands like an industrial tomb.

"On coming home I was working on many local jobs, including Grimsby's new shopping precinct. Again linking up with lads from Harold Street – Paddy Burke, Steve Woodliff and Nigel Allard.

"After two years the work was coming to an end. Once again I was back on the docks at a company on the North Wall called Seabay.

"The foreman was pretty curt with me saying he didn't want any messing about and that there was absolutely no chance of any weekend work. The reality was that I worked twelve consecutive weekends and remained there sixteen years.

"After working nights, I got a call to go back to work late morning for a mass meeting in the canteen. Again, I had an inkling what was coming but closure was still a shock. The Chairman was in the car park and said to me "Paddy, how has it come to this?" I thought I work on night hygiene, I expect you as the Chairman to have a bit more insight than me into this disaster. It was double trouble for us as my wife also worked at the factory and we were made redundant on the same day.

"The tightly knit world of Grimsby Fish Dock again delivered for me and after six further years of employment a loss of orders from the supermarket giant Morrisons meant I was redundant again.

"After a row with the foreman I was pleased to leave and took a life changing decision. I went self-employed specialising in painting and decorating, gardening and window cleaning. I definitely prefer it. I like talking to customers and feel relaxed and get real job satisfaction. My wife has always been an excellent cook and also started her own very successful catering business. I like the flexibility and variety and you can work around your lifestyle and commitments."

Politically Paddy has seen first-hand the way Polish and East European nationals have been treated by local employers. However, like the majority of Grimsby he voted "leave" in the recent referendum "So we could run our own country".

He always votes Labour as do the entire family "Because they are for the working class and this should not be forgotten". Of the Tories he does not sit on the fence – "They probably despise me and I certainly despise them!"

Paddy is part of a very strong and hospitable family. His two daughters have both done well. Katie is Manager at Boots Pharmacy and Paddy says she had a very good start at school in Strand Street with small classes.

Becky who went to Sheffield University is a Manager at the Health Authority dealing with Alzheimer's.

On Grimsby today, Paddy says "There has been a total lack of investment on the East Marsh. As for school leavers it's different, if you weren't academic you went to sea or worked down dock. The better educated got a trade. Today these options hardly exist."

"MY PERSONALITY CHANGED OVERNIGHT" - DEBBIE WALSH
80 TUNNARD STREET, 1971 – 1976

It was a smashing upbringing. We all knew each other and played together. Denise Cribb, Julie Crowther and Sue Brown all lived in our street and we were great mates. We used to go shopping for the older folks in the street, it was a very caring community.

Everyone was "aunty" or "uncle". I've always been a grafter. At 13 I was working at the fish shop over the road and I worked at Asda Wednesday and Friday nights and all day Saturday. I started off shelf stacking but I've always been pretty good with figures and I moved into the Accounts Department.

The first few years at school went very smoothly for me and I enjoyed all aspects. This all changed abruptly when I reached the age of fourteen. I had a very bad fall down a flight of stairs and was really shaken up. According to my mum my whole personality changed overnight. I started missing school and causing trouble and was totally selfish. This was not a passing phase, it continued into my thirties and then I calmed down, I became very close to my Mam again and I was a great deal happier in myself.

I started work at Associated Fisheries where my Dad worked the minute I left school. I was packing fish but after four years I left with repetitive strain injury in my wrist. This was a blow as I loved the job. I was also barmaid at the Fishermans in Cleethorpes and on Friday, Saturday and Sunday at the Excel Club on the East Marsh.

I decided to apply for a job in the kitchen at Butlins, Skegness. I got the job but I found out I was pregnant and left after three months. After the birth of my son Darren I started part time at the Advance Club. I tended to alternate between bar and factory work to try and fit in with childcare arrangements. I definitely prefer bar work, meeting people, and the variety makes it more interesting.

For five years now I have been my Dad's full time carer. I moved around the corner from him so I can respond quickly. It is seven days a week constant effort. All my brothers live away so it all falls on me.

I have lived on the East Marsh virtually all my life. I often feel scared, especially around Rutland Street and I have been mugged twice.

Drugs are at the bottom of most social problems. To root this out I would adopt a far more radical approach and tougher sentencing. The police have been much more active recently.

Debbie has been heavily involved in Harold Street Reunions and the Facebook website.

"We have retained our closeness in adult life. A strong community growing up has kept us together."

"TAKING CARE OF BUSINESS" - MALLY SMITH
(BACHMAN-TURNER OVERDRIVE, 1973)

66 RUTLAND STREET, 1971 – 1976

Mally is testimony to an educational system that completely fails so many working-class children. The "one size fits all approach" of a narrow academic curriculum so often fails to either engage or utilise the interest or potential of huge numbers.

Later in my working life I realised that this waste continues into adult life. Working up in North East England I met a prominent industrialist responsible for the complete revitalisation of an ailing and underperforming factory. His take on the demise of British industry focussed directly on the waste of human potential. His quote made a huge impression on me. "The biggest failure in British manufacturing is our complete inability to get the best out of our people."

Mally has demonstrated in his working life that he has a huge range of practical and technical skills enabling him to successfully run a number of local businesses.

I interviewed Mally in his mobile phone business on Oxford Street in Grimsby. I asked him about his life at school and in the neighbourhood. "It was good, I always enjoyed using my hands and repairing things. Push bikes, motorbikes, anything mechanical. I enjoyed school mainly because of the many characters who attended Harold Street. I really enjoyed their company."

"I effectively left school at fourteen working as a mechanic at my Dad's lock up in Willingham Street. I did the lot, welding, spraying, gearboxes, brakes. I didn't attend school much in my final years. I was a motor mechanic for twenty-four years. I started my own business on Victor Street at thirty-five. After five years I sold my half share in the business and fancied a complete change.

"I certainly did change direction starting as a general dealer on the markets in West Hull. After a while, I was getting fed up with the cold weather and starting work at three in the morning. I spotted an opportunity buying the unlocking gear to enable me to repair and service mobile phones. I took over a semi-derelict shop on Oxford Street and fourteen years later the business is still going strong employing three people."

Mally then went onto outline his other activities.

"I have been on the door at Youngs Restaurant, The Mariners Rest, the Barcelona Night Club and Cottees Bar on Freeman Street."

Anyone who knows Grimsby will testify that this is a list of some of the most challenging venues in the town.

"You get to smell trouble after a while. I always try to be diplomatic and try to diffuse things. Fisticuffs are rare and only if they start.

"When Cottees Bar looked like it was facing closure I bought the lease the day my Mam died."

Mally took me into the rear of his premises and showed me the CCTV of the empty bar at Cottees.

"It pays six people's wages. Weekends are brisk with a good crowd in but weekdays don't generate too much. As long as it pays its way I will continue to run it."

Almost as an afterthought he then mentioned another venture. "I bought a large van and fitted it out as a mobile burger van. I fitted ice cream chimes to it and established a regular round on the Grange and Nunsthorpe estates and of course on the East Marsh. I had a large and loyal customer base and ran this for three years".

Finally I asked Mally to outline the changes in Grimsby over his lifetime.

"Drugs are a major problem and the police are very ineffective. Everything is hard now in a town where jobs were plentiful. There is little discipline. However, I have always enjoyed a good family life."

"LIFELONG LEARNING" - CHRISSY LINES
79 CASTLE STREET, 1971 – 1976

"I grew up in Castle Street in the house that had been passed on by three generations of our family. I was part of a family of nine children. My Dad was a fisherman, but he came ashore after the birth of our third child.

"I had a strict but happy upbringing.

"I loved school. I have always been an avid reader and my ambition was to go to University in order to become a teacher of English. Harold Street taught us life skills. I enjoyed Maths – no calculators then, and Biology. Even at an early age I thought Religious Education was pointless.

"Although I wanted to go on in education to achieve my ambition to become a teacher I had to compromise and acknowledge the reality of my situation. My parents probably would not be able to finance a prolonged period of further and higher education. My two elder sisters were already working in the offices of Christian Salvesens. They alerted me to the position of Office Junior which I successfully applied for.

"I remained for five years and left to have my daughter, Jessica." On returning to work, Chrissy like so many of her era started at one of the fish processing industry's big hitters, Bird's Eye.

"I was there for two years and then started at Ross Group where I was Supervisor for four years. I finished when my marriage ended."

At this point Chrissy decided on a complete change of direction and also reawakened her ambition to progress educationally.

"I wanted to test myself, really see what I was capable of. I enrolled at Grimsby College doing Computer Studies, Human Physiology plus GCSEs in Law and English."

Chrissy's achievements are extremely impressive, she achieved everything she was studying and excelled in Law and English achieving the maximum grades.

"I decided to do voluntary work at Grimsby Hospital doing general clerical duties. When a position in the X-Ray Department came up I got it and worked there for two years."

Chrissy moved onto a supervisory position running and monitoring treatment systems and is involved in a great deal of staff training and development.

I asked her if she regretted not becoming a teacher. She replied,

"Not really, I have continued to develop myself and the staff training gives me a high degree of satisfaction. I enjoy my job and feel I am competent in it.

"However, I still felt the urge to do a degree. I took the plunge and enrolled on a four-year Open University course in Business Management. Initially my motivation was career advancement but by the end the achievement itself was my main motivator."

Chrissy's daughter followed her into working in the Health Service. A stint as a volunteer at the local hospice paved the way for a career in nursing. Firstly as a nurse and latterly as a Complex Care Manager which involves more community-based outreach work.

I asked finally what Chrissy thought of Grimsby then and now.

"The streets were safe, there was a strong community spirit. People looked out for one another. We appreciated what we had, it was hard-earned.

"I wouldn't like to live in my old neighbourhood today. People live in massive pockets of deprivation and many seem defeated and some have given up."

The reasons are depressingly familiar. "A lack of discipline at school. A lack of employment opportunities. Poorly developed social skills, endemic crime and a drug culture blighting so many lives. People leave to go to University and don't come back."

Chrissy brightened and recalled her recent trip to Texas for Andy Dobson's wedding.

"We had a fantastic time, it was just like school forty years ago. Looking around at all my schoolmates from yesteryear I realised what a very strong bond we have and what a strong community we come from."

"SEVEN DAY WEEKEND, UP ALL NIGHT" – JAYNE McLERNON
(LET'S GET ROCKED – DEF LEPPARD)

395 CLEETHORPE ROAD, 1971 – 1976

"I had a happy childhood in a close-knit community. We used to play in the street until the lights came on with parents sat on their front steps talking to friends and neighbours. People looked out for each other.

"I enjoyed school, particularly Domestic Science and History which always interested me.

"The day after I left Harold Street I was packing fish at Chaldurs on the East side of the Royal Dock. I left after three years to go on nights at Bluecrest on Ladysmith Road. It was great, I had no time to spend money during the week and my wage packet didn't take a hammering. I made up for my lack of social activity at the weekends. A typical Saturday's timetable would be as follows. My

Dad would pick me up from work at 6 a.m. on Saturday morning. Home, get changed and at 11 a.m. breakfast at the Pea Bung on Freeman Street market. Home and changed again for the afternoon either at the Mariners Rest, the Mariners Club or the Exchange on Railway Street. My Dad would then take me out for my tea, frequently at the Pea Bung again. Then home, change and out to Cleethorpes in the Dolphin and the Vic before heading up to JD's Nightclub until the small hours.

"I transferred to days after three years on nights, moving on to Findus on Pelham Road and finally transferring to Bird's Eye. I was a barmaid at the Advance Club until it burnt down and then moved to the Corporation Arms. I enjoyed it, it was like being out.

"In 1998 I applied for a job as a Dinner Lady at Strand Juniors. After a while I completed the application forms for Senior Midday Supervisor at the Infants section. I got a rapid result, a phone call asking me, "When can you start?"

"The thing about this job is every day is different. The kids make you laugh and at other times it is the longest two hours of my life."

Jayne is not the sort of person to let the grass grow under her feet.

"In addition I am a cleaner at Boyes, 6 a.m. to 8 a.m. five mornings a week.

"When I look at Grimsby today I think it has undergone massive changes with drugs and low-level crime a daily menace. I feel sorry for today's school leavers, too many have few aspirations. Personally I don't always feel safe in the street where I live."

Jayne's massive achievement is the setting up of the Harold Street site on Facebook. She is the driving force that has achieved over four hundred members, across generations, and from all walks of life.

She organises reunions with terrific attendances even today from a school that closed its doors in 1976.

I asked Jayne why she thought this unique situation continues. "We are bigger and better than other schools because we were so close knit, at school and in the neighbourhood."

Jayne was also part of the Texas Posse attending Andrew Dobson's wedding. The next reunion, at the Casablanca Club in September promises to be the biggest in years.

"OVER THE MARSH" - ANGIE WILSON
151 ALEXANDRA ROAD

Angie is Garry Foster's partner. She did not grow up on the East Marsh as she lived on the West Marsh. This had certain disadvantages as she felt she tended to miss some after-school activities and obviously youth clubs.

"My parents separated when I was eleven and I stayed with my Dad. He was a strict and not particularly loving man. My eldest sister took on the role of Mam.

"I started work at a sweets and tobacconists on Corporation Road. I did three evenings and Saturday and Sunday afternoons and kept it up for eight years, continuing even after gaining full-time employment. It wasn't all work, when Grimsby Leisure Centre opened in 1974 I loved ice-skating and trampolining.

"At school unusually I loved Maths and all sports except swimming. After Harold Street I went to Heneage to do GCSEs. I was successful in Maths, English and Biology and I gained an RSA in Office Practice.

"I applied for a job I saw advertised in the Grimsby Telegraph for an Accounts Clerk/Office Junior at Mac Fisheries. I was there five years until I was made redundant. I took a temporary job at Granada TV Rentals but then stopped work for six years. My husband had an HGV repair and service garage. I started doing the books and parts delivery and progressed to Credit Controller. I did this for eighteen years before leaving for a three years stint as Credit Controller at the Grimsby Telegraph.

"Once again redundancies were in the offing so I went to PD Ports as Accounts Controller only ironically to be made redundant once again.

"I am currently at Five Star Fish as Credit Controller and it is a very intense and high-pressured job."

Angie is rightfully very proud of her two daughters who have done very well.

"One of my daughters is a solicitor locally and my other daughter is an accountant who is responsible for all the non-food products at Asda's Head Office in Leeds.

"I open the post and often see applications from school leavers. I am all too frequently surprised at how poorly presented they are. Both standards of written and oral communication skills seem to have declined in my opinion."

Trying to end on a more upbeat note, Angie observed.

"People are amazed at the very strong bond we maintain with all our old school mates. We went to Texas and regularly meet socially and at school reunions."

"NOT THE GRIMSBY I GREW UP IN" - KARON KENNINGTON
135 RUTLAND STREET, 1969 – 1974

"When I look back I realise what a very happy childhood I had. There wasn't much money about, but we made our own fun, playing in the neighbourhood, I don't remember any trouble. I made life-long friends, it was such a close-knit community. My Dad was a filleter and my Mam was a cleaner. They bought their house in 1967 – the house that my great grandmother had lived in. That's how it was, with first and second generations only living doors away. The neighbours were great, the area bustled with life and there were corner shops everywhere.

"Going to Harold Street was frankly a terrifying experience. On the first day we waited in the passage opposite the main entrance until the bell went before going in. Daft really because once we got in we knew most people anyway.

"I didn't mind school, I enjoyed RE and Cookery. Stand out memories were a trip to Belgium and a week at North Sea Lane camp.

"I think today's school leavers would be genuinely shocked at how I got my first job. The Careers Officer came to school with a batch of job cards. My friend Diane Vincent was interested in fashion and chose the card for Binns. I was successful in gaining employment at Lawson and Stockdale in the food hall along with my schoolmates Lyn Skipworth and Karen Wragg. I was there five years and I loved it. Although Maths was not my strong point at school I got my head around things and did all the evening cashing up.

"On a bit of a whim really I left for Findus with the promise of better money and shorter hours. I was only there a year and couldn't settle. Six to ten wasn't enough hours and you couldn't rely on 10 – 2 being added regularly. I started at Grimsby Hospital as a cleaner and doing the serving of meals and teas and coffees on the OAP's ward. I left to have my first child. My husband is a diver and we met in the Dolphin pub in Cleethorpes.

"Looking back I'm glad I grew up when I did. People now spend an awful lot of time looking at screens. I think there is much less interaction and it has made many less friendly and open.

"We moved my Dad out of Rutland Street in 2008. Basically he was frightened by the vandalism and crime. He became a virtual recluse in his own home. It's not the Grimsby I grew up in."

"COLLAPSING FROM WITHIN" - ROB ROWNTREE
243 WELLINGTON STREET, 1969 – 1974

"We used to roam all over the East marsh. Playing in Salvesen's Pallet Yard on the giant stacks and endless games of football on "Hardy's Rec", Clee Fields and Grant Thorold Park. The highlights of my school life were meeting Tony McLernon and other good mates and some of the staff, Mr McKinell especially, he had a great sense of humour.

"We were frequently involved in what I would call anti-social behaviour. Two stories stick in my mind. One night, on my instigation, we crept into a back garden. It was pitch black. There were almost forty of us. For some reason best known to ourselves we decided to try to push the garden shed over. We pushed and heaved and suddenly I had an inkling it was about to collapse. Collapse it did making an unbelievable racket. Lights went on all over the house and laughing hysterically we all tried to get out through the narrow gate and down the back passage before the irate occupants got out.

Another incident had quite a long build up. For some weeks every time I ran down a back alley I kicked the gate to annoy a small yapping dog. Running down one day with a gang of mates I give the gate my usual prod. "Call that a kick" said one of my mates who shall remain nameless. With that he took a flying leap and pinned the gate back on its hinges. The small yapping terrier had been replaced by a gigantic snarling attack dog who only had eyes for him. Our escape was more of an adrenalin surge than usual.

"When I left school I worked at Abbey Cleaners but after two months I went fishing. I have always had problems with my eyes and therefore my job was as a galley boy below deck. I made three trips altogether but I didn't really take to it.

"Seeing the Northern Lights was a fantastic experience but twenty-two days at sea, eighteen of them with severe weather didn't compensate.

"I had to keep twenty-two crew fed and peeled three buckets of potatoes every day.

"I always wanted to repair TVs but problems with my eyes restricted me again. I had a series of jobs at Clover Dairies, Norman Packaging. My biggest disappointment was when I applied to be a Guard on British Rail. The wage for those days was good but after being successful at interview, I failed the eye test.

"I then worked in a series of labouring jobs which were physically hard. Labouring on building sites and oil refinery shutdowns cleaning out tanks. I started with the Council cleaning gardens and houses and my final job was as a cleaner in the multi-storey flats off Freeman Street. I had to have an eye test every three months and eventually I had to acknowledge the inevitable and take retirement. I have joined the Jehovah's Witnesses and have a good family life.

"The East Marsh has changed and for the worse. Drugs, violence and anti-social behaviour blight this community. My lad is at Primark. He works 32 hours per month. He doesn't pay tax. That's how you get a "jobs miracle" – four/five jobs created where really the hours are consistent with one full-time genuine job. This community is being hollowed out, it's collapsing from within."

"THE BEST CHRISTMAS PRESENT EVER" - STEWART WILLETT
154 RUTLAND STREET, 1971 – 1976

"Looking back it was great. There wasn't much money about but we were happy. We were very active compared with kids now. We walked everywhere. We knocked on doors to see who was coming out – no mobile phones then. Football on Grant Thorold Park, pick the teams and we were away, absorbed for hours. In the summer we switched to cricket. Baz Johnson, John Milson, Graham Stiffel and John Taylor were all great mates.

"At school I really enjoyed Metalwork and Technical Drawing – a good job given my choice of career when leaving. I hated Geography and vowed not to take the leaving exam. In fact I was laid in bed at home when Mr Fretwell came to our house and frogmarched me into the exam room!

"On leaving school, I went to college on an EITB apprenticeship as a sheet metal worker. Our primary customers were Seine Netters, inshore fishing boats. By 1980, this market was in free-fall and I moved to British United Trawlers (BUT) working on their fleet of what was known locally as the Cat Boats – the Ross Jaguar, Ross Puma, Ross Leopard etc. Following the industry's rather cynical practices I was finished the day I completed my apprenticeship."

Stewart was obviously a first class tradesman who was never out of work for very long. Indeed his working life is littered with examples of firms and former managers approaching him to join them.

"After a two-year stint at RJ & A Metalworkers I joined Jex Engineering. Here I worked all over the country with some of the biggest firms in Britain – Kelloggs, Cadburys, Findus, Terrys and Rowntrees. It meant being away from home all week and virtually being embedded in the company when the projects were particularly long running.

"I then worked for two other firms before returning to Jex till 2009 when I was made redundant. It was at this time I started having real problems with my left hand following years of repetitive heavy work. Whilst I eventually returned to work after a long absence I was beset by further health problems. While at Mersline Engineering I was plagued by a persistent sore throat. A course of antibiotics didn't shift it and I knew deep down something was wrong. I was diagnosed with cancer and started an intensive course of chemotherapy followed by radio therapy at Castle Hill Hospital in Hull.

"I finally got the all clear two days before Christmas 2015. I can honestly say it was the best Christmas present I ever had. I go back for six weekly checks which have now been extended to four monthly examinations. That is the good news, but unfortunately the amount of chemotherapy I have had has affected my legs and feet and my mobility is poor. They are not sure whether this situation is permanent or not."

I asked Stewart for his views on Grimsby then and now.

"I grew up on the East Marsh and when I got married moved into Weelsby Street until 2006 – 26 years in all. It was great but latterly it started to deteriorate. Houses were bought up by landlords who weren't too particular about their tenants. I now live in a nice bungalow in Cleethorpes.

"The economy locally has changed, as has the march of technology. I don't see wind technology as a real driver of employment as the volume manufacturing is all located in Hull.

"When I look back, the 1980s were absolutely booming in my industry. All the food halls in factories had to have stainless steel and I used to work some phenomenal hours.

"Today the advent of automated CAD systems and laser cutters have totally deskilled the job and therefore the employment opportunities. The food industry is very volatile, the supermarkets are ruthless, and firms come and go in this town".

"STILL CRAZY AFTER ALL THESE YEARS" – CHRIS MOODY
(SIMON & GARFUNKEL, 1976)

18 COMBER PLACE, 1971 – 1976

"It was fantastic on the East Marsh then. It was exciting as a kid to walk down Freeman Street and see all the fishermen, we saw some sights! On to the market which was absolutely packed, roller skating around the square, it all seemed so vibrant and full of life.

"In all the five years I walked to school our route never deviated. It was almost a point of pride that we never took the main roads, always the alleyways down through the Fisherman's Mission and ending up on Castle Street. We had the same gang of mates, Ronnie Spence, Rob Wraith, Steve Hall, Garry Foster, Winston Thomas, Mick Steer and Nigel Milner.

"When I knew I was going to Harold Street I was worried to death and cried on the morning of the first day. My elder brother gave me the hard word and said stop acting like a baby and get to school.

"Funnily enough I really loved RE, I enjoyed Geography, and English with Mr Robinson always held my interest. The highlight for me were the school dinners which I thought were excellent. I always enjoyed History with Miss Snowden and Mr Foulkes and Mr Rowley were great for Sports and PE."

Chris has had a long career as a local musician and explained how he got started at Harold Street.

"I wanted to join the school band and I fancied the trumpet. Our music teacher, Jack Hall, said "The trumpets are all taken lad, you'll play this." It turned out to be a giant euphonium. I spent more time polishing the thing than playing it. His rule was that every time you played a wrong note you had to do press ups. Luckily I retained a life-long interest in music and all those press ups certainly made me a more effective rugby player.

"My first job after school was at Chattertons skinning dogfish. I stank and so did the whole place. When I had a bath there were fish scales all over the surface of the water. It got so bad that it seemed to penetrate my skin. It's always been a bit of a tradition that you go back to school when you've settled into work and see the staff and tell them how you're getting on. There was a gang of us and although I had clean jeans and shirt on within a few minutes people were sniffing and looking about. My Dad encouraged me to stick at it and get some money behind me before joining the

Merchant Navy. I joined the Navy in 1976 and had seven years at sea. I certainly saw the world, Canada, Vancouver Island, Washington State, Boston, New York and the Eastern Seaboard. I've sailed the Panama Canal down to the West Indies, Saudi Arabia and Japan.

"I came ashore basically because I was getting married. For fifteen years I worked at Salvesens Cold Store on Ladysmith Road. In 1997 following my divorce I remarried. I met Sue my wife originally in 1975 on a Harold Street trip to Aviemore in Scotland. It was a joint visit with Harold Street and Heneage. I then had a stint of agency work primarily driving jobs until in 2003 I secured a job with Novartis my current employer. Initially I did all the post and although self-taught, computer maintenance and servicing.

"Today I act primarily as a Lab Assistant handing the chemical supplies to all the laboratories and also the collection of laundry and its clean replacement to all factory buildings.

"Looking back Grimsby was a much nicer looking place, I used to think it was like a village. Where we lived many of the older people had vivid memories of the war. They were very tolerant of us, many were good gardeners and allowed us to take vegetables home for our mums. There was real community spirit but we rarely ventured far. Trips to Cleethorpes were a really big deal. Martin Cockram used to make cheese and tomato sauce sandwiches and we'd all go down to the boating lake and the arcades. Me and Ronnie Spence used to go to his auntie's in our dinner break from school for a spot of TV and tea and biscuits. We did this every day for three years.

"Today parts of Grimsby are scary. Crime and drugs break the community's spirit. My partner was involved in the Family Intervention Project which did excellent work promoting parenting and related skills. It is now closed due to Government funding cuts. It is all so short-sighted.

"Nothing has replaced the huge infrastructure around fishing and its related industries. It has been totally minimalised. Grimsby seems a smaller place, almost miniaturised since those days when everyone worked, everyone had a job."

Chris then took me upstairs to a room he has dedicated to his music. Posters of The Beatles, The Stones, Status Quo, Thin Lizzy, Gary Moore along with his very impressive collection of guitars and records are everywhere.

"I've gigged with bands all over Lincolnshire and Yorkshire, it's given me a massive buzz all my life."

I DRIVE A BMW BUT I'M STILL A SOCIALIST" - GARRY FOSTER
44 HILDYARD STREET, 1971 – 1976

"I had what I would call a very traditional, working class upbringing. My Mam met my Dad whilst they were both working at the old Hewitts Brewery. My Mam gave up work to bring up the family. It was a very insular life, people didn't stray much from the East Marsh. During my teenage years I would say that my main interests were chasing birds and drinking booze. I regularly frequented the Tower Snooker Hall on Freeman Street. We dabbled a bit in street drugs but it was tame stuff by today's standards. My interest in music is maintained today but seventies heavy rockers Led Zeppelin, Black Sabbath, Free and Bad Company remain my favourites.

"Overall I didn't particularly like school. I felt I had little advice from my parents and generally felt challenged. As I grew older my confidence increased. I was always tall for my age and a certain amount of bravado was required to cement my place in the pecking order. I was big mates with Martin Cockram and Steve Hall and Geography and Art were the subjects I enjoyed most.

"On leaving school at 16 in May I tried very hard to get a start as an electrician but just couldn't open the door. I applied for a job at Dolan's Garage in Scartho as a motor mechanic. I was called to interview and remember walking to the other end of town in my best clothes on one of the hottest days of the year. The place was packed when I arrived for interview, in total there were 127 applicants as I later found out.

"On reflection the interview went really well, I was asked a question about logarithms and answered word perfect. I was offered the job and served a full mechanical apprenticeship being employed for seven years until the garage closed.

"I then had two very bad experiences in short succession. I had three weeks with Joe Frater and three months at Hartwell Ford before a row with the foreman meant I'd had enough and left.

"I decided on self-employment and got a lock up on Wintringham Road. To keep the money coming in I was also working nights packing and blast freezing fish. I applied for jobs in 1986 and secured a position at John Roe Toyota. During this time the Parts Manager was off work ill and I filled in for him. I found the variety interesting and got my head around it very quickly. Eventually I took over as After Sales Manager. I learned the entire commercial side of the business from product knowledge of parts, customer service and the entire system of billing and invoicing.

"My confidence grew, I felt I had a complete grasp of the entire process. Throughout this period I continued to develop myself and went on courses to accredit my skills."

"The financial crash of 2007 – 8 had a devastating effect on the industry and on me personally.

"I had always felt that my pay never matched my performance and after 22 years events dictated a redundancy exercise. I went through this with my entire team and was also a victim of this process.

"Frankly I was very bitter. I had put my heart and soul into my job and tried to run the business as if it was my own.

"After a period taking stock and quite a bit of fishing, I got a job as After Sales Manager at Inchcape at Burton on Trent. After a year I was offered a job as General Manager at Toyota Sudan. My remit was to supervise the setup of the entire operation. I was based in Khartoum and used to go for a drink in the British Embassy. The construction of the garage was the equal on completion of anything in the UK. I had a lovely apartment and a good team around me. During one of the holidays we drove across the Nubian Desert to the Red Sea. The beaches were perfect, unspoiled and undeveloped. We got arrested by the police but a few phone calls from men of influence smoothed out the situation. We met some locals and went boat fishing, cooking everything we caught.

"On returning home, I met a guy at a barbeque who told me about a job at BMW Scunthorpe and I have now been there seven years."

When I asked Garry about Grimsby then and now his views were very radical and very perceptive.

"I was a political animal verging on Communist. Capitalism and especially the Thatcher years were a huge waste of so many people's lives. The rundown of fishing and its consequences have parallels with the mining industry's decimation.

"I am not against change, but if things are going to get worse before they get better then it needs careful and sensitive handling. Change needs planning and gradual implementation to avoid threatening the social fabric. I drive a BMW and live in a nice house in a good area, but the trappings of capitalism haven't altered my socialist beliefs. I believe you look after your fellow man and to avoid crippling communities there needs to be a moral aspect to economic decisions."

Seeing where the interview was going, I asked Garry what he thought of Jeremy Corbyn.

"Corbyn is a principled politician. I am not sure he is strong enough and I am disappointed with the calibre of some Labour politicians."

Finally, Garry asked me a question. "Who do you think has been the greatest man of the twentieth century?"

Before I could answer, he said "It's got to be Nelson Mandela, hasn't it? Well I can pay no higher tribute – John Ellis of the Shalom Youth Club is Grimsby's Nelson Mandela."

"HAROLD STREET TO HAUTE COUTURE" - JULIE JENSEN

COMBER PLACE, 1971 – 1976

My Dad was a Danish fisherman. He lived in Hull where he was previously married. When he started sailing out of Grimsby he met my Mam. In a locality of big families, I was unusual in that I was an only child. I had a very happy childhood playing out all day and largely making our own entertainment. We moved into Comber Place as newly built houses. Everyone knew each other, unlike today.

"I got a real shock and was very upset when I got a letter informing me that I was going to Harold Street. I wanted to go to Havelock and thought it would be really rough.

"There were no half measures with me. I hated Maths and we would try to get Mr Seedall talking about his war exploits, anything to side-track him. I didn't like Art either but I loved Homecraft.

"The first lesson in the kitchens always followed the same ritual. You had to clean the ovens. I was hard at work when Mr Fisher, passing through said "Put some elbow grease into it Julie". When I asked where it was, he replied "Try that big cupboard". I couldn't find any, he said "Here's a penny, see if you can buy some over the weekend". On Monday morning I went to the chemist on the corner of Harold Street and Rutland Street. It was a place where lots of gossiping women congregated. To howls of laughter, I was told there was none in stock.

"I left school the third week in May on a Friday. By Monday I was at Ross's on the Fish Finger Line along with six other girls from Harold Street. I didn't really like factory work and after three years switched to shop work at the old Jackson Grandways store on Park Street. After five years I left to get married and had two kids.

"My second child, Ashley was born on a Saturday and by the following Saturday I was working part-time serving fish and chips at the Fisherman's Catch on Grimsby Road. I became Manageress and handled all aspects from making fishcakes to all the wet side hygiene and stock control. Bob the owner moved back to Denmark and I was on the move again after ten years.

"I was back at Ross's again but this time as a Team Leader. But things had changed, there was a lot more pressure to do more with less and the atmosphere was much harder-edged. The hours and shift work were taking their toll on family life and I switched back into retail. In fact I had two part-time jobs, at Tesco and also British Telecom – which I absolutely loved. We dealt with Directory Enquiries from London and Newcastle. Apart from dealing with a load of Geordies we could barely understand it was very good. I was very sorry when it shut down but then simply topped up my hours at Tesco.

"After fourteen years at Tesco I started training as a nail technician."

I never expected the last section of this interview, as Julie described a truly remarkable six-year journey.

"I have been running my own business for six years from customised premises at my own home. I have had a fantastic time.

"I posted photographs of a set of nails I had worked on on Facebook. I received a reply from Marion Newman one of the world's leading nail technicians asking me how I had achieved such outstanding results. I explained my technique and thought that was all there was to it. She got back to me asking me to join her team at London Fashion Week. This quickly progressed to Paris Fashion Week with "A" Listers and supermodels as clients. I have been working in Los Angeles on the TV series "Botched" about plastic surgeons in LA and did all the nails and make up.

"I can count Vivienne Westwood, Rita Ora, stars of the X Factor and Strictly Come Dancing as my clients. Also I am involved in the Cannes Film Festival.

"Sometimes I think little old me from Harold Street has done all this.

"I went with the Texas Posse to Andy Dobson's wedding. All of us went to Harold Street. School was the best time of my life. We have been left forty-one years and we still meet up regularly. People made it what it was, we were like one big family.

"Grimsby today is blighted by a lack of opportunities. I've seen a different side of life working in London. I like the variety and mix of cultures. Now when I get off the train at Kings Cross I almost feel like I'm coming home. The work is down there and realistically I could see myself moving south.

"Obviously if this happened I would miss my friends and family, especially my old school mates who have been absolutely brilliant when I needed support in my life."

"NOW I FEEL MORE LIKE A SOCIAL WORKER" - DIANE SANFORD
172 WEELSBY STREET, 1971 – 77

"Growing up on the East Marsh was a good experience for me. It was a friendly place where everyone knew their neighbours and there was a genuine community spirit where people looked out for one another."

Diane then dropped in a real bombshell and showed me graphically just how much things have changed.

"My mum worked on the 2 – 6 shift at Bird's Eye. She used to leave the door unlocked for us coming home from school. It was never a problem.

"Most of the time I used to just hang around with my mates and watch the lads play football in Grant Thorold Park. I liked school, mainly for the social aspects and particularly enjoyed English with Mr Robinson and Art with Mr Whatley. Mr Peacock frankly frightened me to death!

"I started work as a machinist at Havelok Knitwear on Wintringham road. Both my sisters worked there and it was hard graft, piece work. I left after a year. I was pregnant with my first child and moved in with my Mum and Dad on the Willows Estate. In 1980 two years later I got married and moved to a house in Weelsby Street. I started work at United biscuits part-time as a machine operative. By 1981 I was having my second son and I started at Bird's Eye. The job, boning fish, was particularly horrible, we were generally soaked and smelled of fish, but looking back we had some real laughts in the Wet Shed. When my daughter was born in 1984 I stayed at home until she was ready for full time nursery. I then started a very long association with Weelsby Street Primary School. Firstly I started volunteering at the nursery two afternoons a week. Then I became a Dinner Lady, finally I was offered the job of Teaching Assistant and have now completed twenty-eight years in the role."

Diane is obviously well placed to give a real insight into the changes of the decades since leaving school.

"The majority of kids are absolutely fine. Unfortunately a minority, a growing minority, are frankly out of control. The abuse can be awful, remember this is a primary school we are talking about.

"I used to love this job, but the last few years, more and more I feel like a social worker.

"Additionally we have problems with children in that their first language is not English.   Russians, Poles, Lithuanians and Romanians, although generally they are well behaved."

I asked Diane to account for the deterioration over the years. Her replies were now becoming depressingly predictable.

"We have landlords who bulk buy houses and have no interest in offering a decent standard of service.   This leads to a situation where they will accept virtually anybody.   Drugs are endemic and family situations challenging. Some seem to lack any real aims or a purpose in life, which inevitably leads to a lack of self-esteem, pride and self-respect. In an area once renowned for people who worked hard in tough jobs I'm not sure some actually want work."

To balance the picture I asked Diane to try to finish with some positivity and optimism.

"There are many decent people on the East Marsh who keep their homes immaculately and clearly are fed up with the way things are. Unfortunately they are stuck, moving is a difficult option.   The police could be a great deal more effective than they are in my opinion."

"DO THINGS WITH MY HANDS THAT MOST MEN CAN'T" – JOHN MILSON
(HARD WORKIN' MAN, BROOKS & DAMN)

18 GUILDFORD STREET, 1971 – 1976

"I loved growing up in the community. We roamed all over, the freedom made it a very carefree and fun time. I was always heavily into all sports alongside my great mates Les Gibney and Glen Wilson.

"Harold Street always had a reputation, it was a hard, strict school. While I appreciate some aspects of the discipline were necessary and I have many good memories, some aspects were negative and unfair. I was in all the school teams and enjoyed metalwork and biology. With some of the weaker teachers you tended to switch off or play up learning very little. Some teachers gave up and didn't bother much either. As with most things you responded to staff you liked and respected and in subjects you enjoyed or excelled in.

"I have been a builder for 40 years. My first interview was conducted on the back doorstep of my future employer's house. I joined Alan Wiseman builders and was part of a four-man team. I was employed as a trainee bricklayer, but also learned plastering, tiling and roofing. This stood me in good stead as today you need to be not only multi-skilled but proficient in a number of trades.

"The recession in 1984 sent a shockwave through the building industry. We were heavily involved in Grant work and this simply dried up. Money just stopped coming in and I had no option but to go self-employed. For about two years I kept going but I seemed to be averaging only about three days a week. Mick Staples came around and offered me a job and it went well for six years. Once again the economy was again on a downturn and his workforce went from twenty to two. I was finished, and for the first time in my life, out of work.

"I was offered a job with the Council and after initially being reticent, decided to take it. We were mainly involved in building garden walls and kitchen and bathroom upgrades on the Nunsthorpe Estate. I loved it and surprisingly the money wasn't bad either. The only drawback was that your employment was terminated when budgets ran out.

"I then had no option but work on my own and some of the winter months were very hard.

"I was offered a permanent job with the council and when the housing stock was transferred to the management of Shoreline, worked for them. I was then transferred to Mears but Shoreline took the contract back in-house when VAT went from 15% to 20%. It was now more viable to operate in-house.

"Obviously I now have more job security and a pension. I have major problems with my knees. I specialise in disabled adaptions to bathrooms and I am constantly on my knees.

"Being out and about in Grimsby working I see many problems first hand. I see many first-class people who try to make things right for their families. The other side is depressing, parents with beer cans at 8 in the morning and ignoring or shouting at their kids on the way to school. Constant use of mobiles shuts out society and technology is certainly not always a boon.

"The pride has gone out of too many people in Grimsby."

"REACH OUT I'LL BE THERE" – MELANIE HARROWER
(THE FOUR TOPS, 1967)

15 RAVENSPURN WAY, 1971 – 1976

"I originally lived on the East Marsh on Strand Street but we moved when I was eleven, just as I started Harold Street."

Unlike the majority I have interviewed, Melanie did not have a very happy early childhood.

"I had a rough time prior to going to Harold Street. My job was to look after my younger brother Kingsley who was mixed race and had both physical and learning disabilities. My opportunities to mix and have a normal childhood were limited. I lived in the flats and it was a very close-knit community. People looked out for one another and shared. If someone was ill it didn't take long before they would get a home-made pie or a parcel of fish.

"Obviously Harold Street's reputation meant I was fed a diet of horror stories and I was absolutely petrified at starting there. I couldn't have been more wrong, school was a revelation and the best years of my life. Mrs Blades took me under her wing and nurtured me through school. I loved English, History and Home Economics and Music. I hated Maths. I made some fantastic friends Jayne McLemon, Pat Hammond, Sharon Codd and Julie Cottam.

"I left school on the Friday and started the following Monday at St Hughes' Nursing Home on £16 per week. My burning ambition was to become a nurse and go to Africa and work with children. After two years I applied to Grimsby Hospital and passed all the tests and the interview. Just as I was leaving the man interviewing me said, "How tall are you Melanie?" I said I didn't know but when he measured me his face fell. I was under the five-foot limit set by the hospital. Luckily Louth County Hospital had no such ruling and I started my training there as an SEN. Eighteen months into my two-year course I discovered I was pregnant and obviously had to leave. I was married five weeks later.

"Two years later I needed some new windows, so I started on the Pizza Line at Birds Eye on the 6 – 10 shift.

"For two years I was a full-time mum of two and I then went to work at St Margaret's Nursing Home as a Physiotherapist's Aid. I also did night sitting with elderly patients working all night from 7 p.m. to 7 a.m. Fridays and Saturdays.

"I started at Old Clee Primary School as a Teachers Aid working with deaf children. I loved the job but it was only covering for maternity leave. After two years doing supply work I secured a permanent post. The job was working with SEN pupils. I was there for three happy years and worked predominantly one to one with a deaf pupil. Once he was ready to leave it meant my job effectively disappeared and I was made redundant.

"I got a job with Mencap working with adults with learning disabilities in a home environment. We took them out to socialise and on holidays but basically it meant round the clock care. I worked there for fourteen years but when my eldest went to Leeds university I transferred back into schools in order to fit around my youngest daughter of eight.

"I started at Cambridge Park Academy in 2003. It is a special school with 200 on roll. I work one to one with a pupil who has physical disabilities and uses a wheelchair. I love the job and the kids make it special. I get real job satisfaction. Even after all these years I till look after my younger brother. I think my formative years really equipped me to do this job.

"Major changes have taken place in schools since I started. I think it has become less child-centred with the huge emphasis on paperwork, gathering evidence and the whole process of accountability. Obviously there is less freedom and scope for displaying initiative. Everything has to be recorded and validated. It has its place but I believe the pendulum has swung too far. Luckily we have an amazing team of staff here at the school."

Melanie recently achieved excellent marks in taking her GCSE English examinations, testimony to her determined character and the stamina and empathy she has shown in a long career of helping others.

PHOTOS – THE SEVENTIES

Shalom Youth Club Members

"They took some working with, they were tough – tougher than kids today."

"Three Day Millionaires"

Ready to go ashore, wages in my hand,

Brand new suit, I guess I've no real plans.

Garry Foster and the late Martin Cockram

Stanley Street, 1977

PHOTOS – THE EIGHTIES

Freeman Street – "the Fishermen's Street"

"A vital area full of life"

Tony McLernon & Peter Rowley

On the pontoon, Grimsby Fish Docks, 1984

Trainee Filleters on the Pontoon

Grimsby Fish Docks, 1984

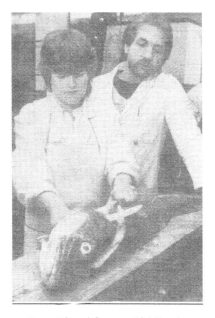

New Blood for an Old Trade

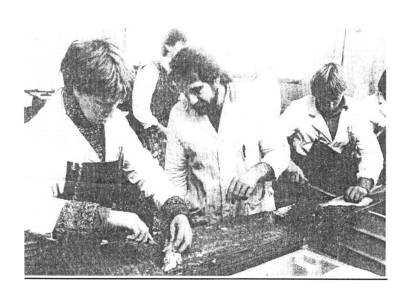

PHOTOS – THE EAST MARSH TODAY

Rutland Street

"Not the Grimsby I grew up in."

The Oasis Garden at Grimsby Community Church

"Built on the Marsh by volunteers"

John Ellis with Club Members outside The Shalom Today

"ANOTHER BRICK IN THE WALL" - BARRY JOHNSON
(PINK FLOYD)

62 RUTLAND STREET, 1970 – 1975

"I only have good memories. All your mates lived only doors away. We loved sport, football in the winter and cricket in the summer on Grant Thorold Park. My great mates were Graham Stiffel, Colin Culyer, Andy Dobson and Stewart Willet.

"I loved Harold Street, we had a cracking school football team. Mr Foulkes was our PE teacher and a great motivator who really knew the game. We won the league championship three years on the trot against local comprehensives who were three times our size. By 1975 we were in the process of merging with Heneage as Harold Street's closure had been made official. PE, Woodwork and Metalwork were my favourite subjects although some of us were thrown out of Metalwork because we refused to have our hair cut.

"I originally wanted to be a joiner. Me and Martin Cockram went to Grimsby Council to do the apprenticeship tests. We also went around all the firms we knew trying to get a start. Apprenticeships were in freefall and this was no easy task. I went down to the job Centre and was sent for an interview at Phil Patterson Builders. I got a start and I was lucky in that he was a good tradesman who taught me all aspects of the job. I think that this practical training was for me far superior than attending college. I became good friends of the family and even today still work with two of his sons.

"I have worked in the trade all my life. Luckily mostly in the Grimsby area. I have worked on a big job in the Lake District on a major barn conversion and in Oxford laying bases for conservatories. The 1979-1980 recession saw me leaving for Germany. I worked in Munich, Dusseldorf, Stuttgart and Cologne and came home just in time for my 21st birthday.

"Grimsby has for me changed beyond recognition. We lived in Rutland Street. My Mam had three sisters who all lived in Rutland Street, another two who lived in Tunnard Street and Daubney Street. That's how close-knit the community was.

"We worked on two properties in Castle Street for a company from Leeds that had bought up 200 houses mainly on the East Marsh. Our job was to convert two up two down terraces into five bedsits.

They are lining their pockets and simply creating massive social problems.

"In 41 years, I've never struggled for work although I've had to go abroad to keep in employment. I don't see many youngsters today who are keen to enter the trade, it's hard physically and you are out and exposed to the elements. I took on my brother-in-law as an apprentice and he did very well, representing the college in competitions.

"I played local football until I was 42. My Dad played for Tartan Forties until his fifties and I even played against him in a cup tie. I now play golf with a handicap of twelve and really enjoy going skiing. School gave me the kick start to enjoy a long career in local sport."

"THE COMMUNITY OF THE EAST MARSH OF 40 YEARS AGO HASN'T GONE AWAY – IT JUST NEEDS NURTURING" - ALAN BURLEY

397 WELLINGTON STREET, 1969 – 1974

"I had a fantastic group of friends growing up, Mick Woodhouse, Wally Kirwin and Paul Revell. Harold Street was the only school I wanted to go to as all my mates were there. My Dad had a job at Dixons Paper Mill and he was always on good wages. At that time, I didn't go to the Shalom Youth Club but spent my time listening to music, playing football and later drinking with my friends.

"Harold Street had a brilliant band under the direction of music teacher Jack Hall and I can still remember to this day listening to them. None of us liked RE and in Woodwork and Metalwork we always seemed to make things that were of no use to anyone. This started a lifelong struggle for me to achieve any competence in DIY!

"My first job was a motor mechanic. I had always enjoyed tinkering with my Dad's car and I got a start at Minto Motors on a five-year apprenticeship at £9 per week. Although I completed my apprenticeship it wasn't long before I realised that this was not what I wanted, in fact I hated it. The firm were good employers and when I completed my indentures even had a little party for me and invited my Mum and Dad. Half an hour before this I told them I was leaving.

"My Dad, who was by now a security guard at Wold Farm Foods was not amused at me packing in a job without having anything to go to. I asked him if there was anything doing at his factory and I started, staying for 22 years. I became interested in Union work and became Site Convener for the GMB in charge of the Stewards Committee. Wold Farm Foods were a very good firm to work for, with good pay and conditions. There was a great deal of ex-fishermen in the factory, but I managed to persuade them that union membership was essential. I was becoming more and more involved politically and I thought that the Council's Food town initiative might be a boost for jobs and growth.

"The recession was a body blow for us. The bottom dropped out of the frozen food market as consumers cut back. We experimented with some bizarre products including chocolate flavoured broccoli to try to break into the children's market. We were taken over by Fisher Foods and with closure rumours rife we were always favourite to go. We closed in the late 1990s with the loss of 220 jobs.

"Building on the experience of earlier mass closures in Grimsby substantial government funding was made available for retraining and upskilling. I didn't take up this opportunity basically because I had no idea what I wanted to do.

"I'd always had an idea that I would like to work with disabled children. A friend had an autistic son and I worked with him for 8 months and supported him at the day centre he attended. This gave me the surety and confidence that this is what I really wanted to do.

"I got a job as a Support Worker with Links Community Trust. The job involved being based in house to develop coping skills and build independence. We moved people on significantly in their lives. I loved the job and accepted more and more responsibility including overnight stays, administering medicine over three years.

"I went for an interview with Cargon who ran a 9-bed housing unit in Cambridge Road, Cleethorpes. The client group were 16 – 24 year olds, often estranged from their families. Many had issues around drugs and alcohol.

"Although the interview did not go smoothly, as many of the questions they posed were outside my experience, they offered me the job. When I expressed my surprise, their attitude was we can help you build on the skills and experience you already have. This summed them up, they were excellent employers who paid well and offered plenty of support and training.

"However, I wanted to make a difference and make that difference in the community I grew up in. I became the Labour Councillor for Grant Thorold and Heneage. In my 12 years on the Council I became Chair of Estates and Management, and Chair of Planning. Grimsby Labour Party was dominated by largely right wing and older members. Two very controversial decisions were taken during my stewardship. Firstly the closure of Claremont Care Home and the building of the incinerator. Neither of these decisions were taken lightly and we put in a great deal of time and effort to get to what I still believe were the correct decisions. However, many councillors, myself included were subject to vicious personal attacks.

"Looking back on my time as a councillor there are many cases of assisting people that I take a great deal of satisfaction from. One severely disabled girl required a stairlift and walk-in shower conversion which we manged to secure for her. Whilst in her house I noticed a picture of Glen Hoddle. Ironically Grimsby Town were drawn against Chelsea in the Cup. I phoned Chelsea Football Club and asked for a signed picture of Hoddle. Some days later I got a call from them saying "Make sure she is in at 5.45 p.m." Right on the dot, Glen Hoddle appeared at her door and presented the autographed photo in person!"

When Alan told me this, although I have never been Hoddle's greatest fan, he certainly went up in my estimation.

"I lost my seat when the Liberals and Tories formed a pact. They didn't stand a candidate in my ward to allow the Liberals a clear run. I knew then the writing was on the wall. In twelve years of hard relentless graft we had built the vote to 1100 for Labour. However, the electoral arithmetic meant that the Tories with 800 and the Lib Dems with 400 would just limp over the line. I admit, I was absolutely gutted, I had worked some colossal hours and missed out on my daughter growing up.

"I got a job as a Neighbourhood Engagement worker employed by Shoreline Housing on the Yarborough Estate. The estate was to be pulled down and I got the residents involved in the planning and development of the new one. After a year the funding for my job ran out. When some funding came available for a Community Worker in the East Marsh, I leapt at it. It meant I was now working to build community involvement in my old neighbourhood.

"We initiated a number of developments – a stall on Freeman Street Market as an advice centre and resources pushed into Victor Street Children's Centre. We spotted a major gap with no evening activities so we started evening meals, bingo and dancing. We went into partnership with the charity Foresight and accessed their building. I started writing funding bids and managing volunteers.

Out of the blue I was offered a job to do similar work at the YMCA. I have now been in post over three years and secured over £1 million in funding. This has enabled us to develop a mental health project for young people, a training centre and two youth clubs.

"I hope this is my last job, I love it. I still volunteer and I am proud to be a trustee of the Shalom Youth Club and Harbour Place."

Alan finally summarized his outlook on life.

"When I was 22 I developed a serious condition, which meant I was off work for eighteen months. I was making a slow and painful journey down to the paper shop when I saw a blind man walking with a stick. I immediately stopped feeling self-pity and got a grip of myself. I now live for the day. I don't worry about tomorrow and work in the community. I now feel calm and do not endure stress.

"The community that was in the East Marsh 40 years ago hasn't gone away, it just needs nurturing. It is still full of people who care deeply about the place."

"OUR HOUSE" – JULIE LOVE
(MADNESS, 1982)

47 HILDYARD STREET, 1970 – 1975

Julie has lived in her house all her life, 56 years in total, right in the heart of the East Marsh.

She recalls her childhood.

"The community was very close knit, we never locked doors like we do today. Women scrubbed the steps and swept the front pavement and if you were out and it was raining they would bring in your washing. It was a real community. Virtually all the men worked in the fishing industry, down dock or in the numerous factories that were open then. My Dad worked at Courtaulds."

Julie's education was delivered entirely on the East Marsh.

"I started at Hilda Street Infants at five where I met my lifelong friend Julie Camburn. Then onto Weelsby Street and finally Harold Street Secondary. My Mam was a dinner lady at Weelsby Street. I was the most popular kid in the school. When my mam was serving out dinners at the hatch all my schoolmates said they were my friends in the hope of getting extras.

Julie painted me a picture of more innocent times.

"After school we were outside playing, either in the street, back gardens or Grant Thorold Park. In the summer we used to go and buy a 6d fishing net and go up to Hardy's Recreation Ground to catch newts and frogs. There was a little stream there, long gone, it is now a car park.

"Saturday mornings were the big event of the week. My older brother John took my brother Mark, me and my sister Karen to the Regal Cinema down Freeman Street. 6d to get in and 6d to spend.

"Freeman Street throbbed with activity. Marks and Spences, Woolworths, Shoefayre, the Green Shield Stamp shop and a host of other smaller businesses. Butchers, Bakers, Newsagents, Off Licences, Laundry and Dry Cleaners, Jewellers and Furniture shops.

"When I first started at Harold Street all the desks had inkwells and for a time we used them. At first boys and girls were separated but we soon became mixed.

"The 60s and 70s were a good time to grow up. Life was simpler then – not the technology and pressure there is now or the bullying that seems all too prevalent in schools.

"I enjoyed school, my Mam's oft repeated adage that "They are the best years of your life" were true in my case.

"I left school in the July of 1975 and got a job at Kwik Save in Freeman Street. I got £7 a week and thought that having money and a wage packet was great. After ten months it closed and I was made redundant.

"I then switched to a clothes shop in Cleethorpes and although I hated it I stopped three years. I became a Forecourt Attendant in a petrol service station but again redundancy followed when they went self-service.

"I decided to try factory work. United Biscuits for three years, then onto Ross Youngs for twelve years. Finally, Birds Eye which I really enjoyed, there was a real family atmosphere and the closure announcement in 2004 was a real shock.

"For the past eleven years I have been a Warden in Sheltered Housing Accommodation."

I asked Julie about her neighbours on Hildyard Street.

"My next dour neighbours are Romanians. They are the best neighbours I've ever had."

Julie has been a very good neighbour to them. She has helped with sorting out doctors and dentists, converting driving licences and helped them rectify a grossly inaccurate water bill. She said, "I was hanging out the washing one day and they said to me are you ready, we're having a barbeque in your honour. They wanted to buy the house but the landlord won't sell it – I'll be sorry to see them go."

Julie is a big film fan and is very well travelled but still retains a great deal of affection for the neighbourhood she has lived in all her life. Nevertheless, she has strong views.

"People need to be re-educated. This is where their kids are growing up. We need to massively invest in improving the environment and get more well-paid jobs. This would re-instil a sense of pride and self-worth."

"THE WAY WE WERE"
(BARBRA STREISAND, 1973)

I have now finished the first stage of this story and it is time to take stock, and if possible make some sense, and draw some conclusions.

High profile writers and academics have tried to document the period and explain its economic and social trends. Depending on their particular political views and their areas of interest, they draw interesting and often contradictory finalities.

We are often treated to politicians booming "No return to the seventies". The media portray it as a time of chaos, with rampant union power threatening the entire political order. Dominic Sandbrook in his History of the period, 1970 – 1974, shows his attachment to this view in his title "State of Emergency".

Those political luminaries David Cameron and Boris Johnson took to the airwaves in 2013 with siren warnings about "dragging Britain back to the 1970s".

Cameron said to cheering attendees at the Tory Conference in Manchester, "we'll leave the 1970's style socialism to the others; we are the party of the future."

Boris Johnson in a typically florid statement warned against a "1970's blend of divisiveness and business-bashing and union control."

Ignore the fact that both of these commentators were Eton pupils at the time and were not really in a position to make valid judgements. They merely internalised the Tory version of history that the UK was going to the dogs before being rescued by Margaret Thatcher.

The Strawbs with their 1973 chart hit succinctly summarised this version of events, "You don't get me I'm part of the union." They portrayed the balance of power in society as strongly tilting towards organised labour, "I'm not very hard but the sight of my card makes me some kind of superman."

However in 2004 Jim Jackson from Surrey University assembled what was called a Measure of Domestic Progress to try and calculate whether life has improved or worsened. He drew on calculations from a range of factors including inequality, economic growth, spending on health and education, crime, family breakdown, pollution and other variables.

His conclusion, given the constant drumbeat of right wing politicians and a supplicant media was shattering. The year in which the greatest progress was identified, and Britain was at its happiest, was 1976.

In the 1970s he revealed, despite the upheavals people were a great deal more content. The reasons highlighted point to a society that was far more equal than today's, where outside employment black spots, school leavers would go straight into paid employment. Graduates left university debt-free and housing in terms of affordability was only five times average earnings. Today it is ten times average earnings. State owned utilities may have been subject to a hostile media coverage, but fuel costs were kept relatively low, especially compared to today's privatised energy giants.

Other commentators see this as an age before technology dominated the home, so personal relationships and direct communication were important. Society was far more cohesive than today's atomised and fragmented communities.

Virtually without exception everyone interviewed demonstrated a strong and vivid picture of the East Marsh as a happy and highly integrated community. They are also united in their view that something has been lost that cannot be replaced and that Grimsby today is a diminished place because of it. A community built on physical resilience and the ability to work incredibly hard has vanished. Improvements in individual lives and circumstances cannot seem to compensate for this loss of identity, the abolition of the industry that gave the entire community its meaning. Although it might be said that a sense of nostalgia might dominate many of these narratives there is a consensus that many things of real worth have been forfeited.

2nd September 2017

Harold Street Reunion, Casablanca Club, East Marsh, Grimsby

I attended this reunion, which was a sell out and packed to the rafters. Most of the attendees left over 40 years ago, some fifty and even sixty. The enduring success and obvious enjoyment of these occasions underlines the fact that some things are worth remembering, some things are worth celebrating.

PART TWO 1979 – 1986

THE RISE OF THATCHERISM

Despite denials of a state funeral it was staged amid great pomp with a gun carriage procession from Trafalgar Square to St. Paul's.

Michael Deacon, unsurprisingly a fan, wrote a long piece in the Daily Telegraph headlining "How applause drowned out the jeers." He concluded "This was a day, in short, of tributes untarnished. A day when, to a far greater degree than expected, abuse was overcome by respect, violence by decency, and hatred by love."

Meanwhile the Barnsley Chronicle reported banners and bunting as thousands congregated to celebrate her demise. A horse-drawn effigy was paraded through the village of Goldthorpe in an open coffin and then ceremonially set on fire on waste ground. Celebrations were reported throughout the ex-mining heartlands as though missives from another country.

The landlady of the Rusty Dudley in Goldthorpe said, "It was a brilliant community, really busy, but now everything has gone dead because no-one has any money and there's no jobs."

Another resident, Caroline Woodcock said, "I completely agree what she did was wrong … but this is a person and she's got a right to a peaceful funeral."

In Durham a miner contested this view, "We've shown as much respect to her as she did to us."

Thatcher was divisive, nationally her funeral proved equally controversial. Even in death she divided the nation. What is truly significant however is that unlike the woman herself today her ideas are alive and kicking. The economic collapse following the financial crisis of 2007 – 2008 has not had a great impact on the mettle of Thatcherites. In fact there has been a confident reassertion of its tenets under Osborne. The crisis of Thatcherism has spawned a more Thatcherite Tory Party than that of the 1980s. Its pre-Keynesian prescription of huge spending cuts during a slump have exacerbated and needlessly prolonged meaningful recovery.

By any truly objective assessment Thatcherism was by the goals it set itself a failure. The central objective of economic policy was the control of inflation. Yet after a decade of turmoil inflation in October 1990 stood at 10.9% having been 10.3% in May 1979 when she came to power.

However to have such an enduring legacy means a powerful message must surely transcend such unfortunate facts. Thatcher successfully challenged almost every aspect of the post war settlement and established her beliefs as orthodox common sense, summarized in the uncompromising soundbite, "There is no alternative."

The arrival of the Thatcher government in 1979 marked a decisive departure from the policies and behaviour that were the hallmarks of previous Labour and Conservative administrations. The important issue here is that the Thatcher view did not merely challenge Labour, but crucially the whole thrust of previous Tory governments, particularly the Heath government. Lessons were learned and plans formulated to prevent any repetition of the Heath debacle.

The Thatcherites argued that the whole drift of British society since the early sixties had been for the worse and only drastic action could reverse this decline. They rejected "more of the same" and with both energy and some ability, set about promoting the class interests of British Capital. Through a sustained onslaught on the Trade Union movement and the public sector they aimed to reverse the gains made by the working class to provide a springboard for economic recovery. Low real wages and a disciplined and experienced workforce exposed to the rigours of the market would act as a magnet for investment, crucially inward investment.

"Wealth creators" were not the "horny-handed sons of toil" but entrepreneurs to be encouraged by a low tax environment, unchecked by the dead hand of the state. Investment funding would be available because there was no "crowding out" of funding streams by an ever-expanding public sector. The economics were only part of this transformation programme. Social mores needed to be shifted from a collectivist outlook enshrined in socialism where "an injury to one is an injury to all", to an emphasis on the individual. Thatcher in quoting the parable of the Good Samaritan claimed his altruism was only possible because of his wealth. In an amazing statement she claimed, "There is no such thing as society, only a collection of individuals."

Thus Thatcherite economics aimed to tip the balance of class forces firmly in favour of capital over labour, whilst ideologically challenging the precepts of the Welfare State with a raw focus on individualism.

Superficially there are marked similarities with the early "Selsdon Man" programme of Heath. That Thatcher managed to promote these ideas far more successfully was due to a number of factors.

Firstly Heath and many of his cabinet were luke-warm in much of their free-market fundamentalism, steeped as they were in the post-war consensus. Thatcher gradually surrounded herself with like-minded ideologues – Tebbitt, Sir Keith Joseph and marginalised those relics such as Jim Prior from the Heath era who she dubbed the "Wets". Her yardstick of a colleague was "is he one of us". The result was a determined and ruthless cadre of like-minded individuals who pursued their agenda with energy, skill and commitment.

What Thatcher had and Heath did not was a fundamental and coherent theory to weld together this economic and social programme she propagated. Thus instead of a wide-ranging menu of free-market dogma, it had the intellectual coherence to challenge Keynesianism head on. These facts ensured that when the going got tough there was no "U turn" or retreat on the terrain in which she chose to fight.

The challenge to the whole Keynesian ethos came in the form of monetarism eagerly adopted by hard line right wing Tories. Its high priest was Milton Friedman of the Chicago School of Economics and Hayeck an inspiration from an earlier era. Friedman declared "inflation is always and everywhere a monetary phenomenon".

Having studied historical trends he deduced that an expansion in the supply of money preceded a bout of rising prices, or inflation. Therefore it is all so simple, control the money supply and you control inflation. Britain became a living laboratory to test the durability of the new religion.

But for the wider social and economic transformation sought by the Tories monetarism had other attractions. The brutal logic of monetarism is that it creates the conditions that precipitate a major slump. Why you might ask would any rational government inflict this on the country? Given their view of the crisis of capitalism, radical and extreme shock therapy was essential to set the country on a completely new set of tracks. Lame duck firms would be allowed to go to the wall and the labour shakeout following closure was viewed as a price worth paying. The public sector was to be allowed to shrink or be privatised. Unemployment which approached four million was to be used as a disciplining factor on wages and conditions in the classic Marxist view of the "reserve army of labour. At its peak unemployment was increasing at the rate of 100.000 per month with huge swathes of Britain's manufacturing base decimated. All that was required was that the government held its nerve, kept control of the money supply, and used interest rates as a disciplining tool.

The theory was that after this shock therapy the economy would emerge phoenix-like with "dead wood" companies eliminated and employers on the front foot when dealing with organised labour. Britain could then compete with the best and long-term decline would be replaced by a dynamic environment of business expansion, growth and wealth creation.

That was the theory, what of the reality?

First of all, before any debate about the merits of the causal link between the money supply and inflation, the main policy plank, controlling the money supply, proved difficult. In a modern economy with huge access to all forms of credit and with government policies creating massive increases in welfare payments to the army of unemployed, control became an elusive objective. Continually raising interest rates as an instrument of correction proved to be politically unacceptable.

Perhaps the biggest indictment on economic grounds was the feasibility of such a rupture to an economy in decline. The analogy of a cold shower for a healthy person is apposite as it proves to be invigorating. Apply the same medicine to someone who is ill and it may well make matters even worse. In a nutshell regarding the phoenix and the ashes, the question increasingly being posed was "What if only the ashes are left?"

The economic havoc of the monetarist experiment created devastation, dislocation and misery primarily in the older industrial areas and the manufacturing heartlands. Harshness and despair and a lack of hope and purpose were inflicted on millions. The government response was all too often, justification on the grounds that many industries were "over-manned" or masked in a great deal of "hidden unemployment". The most callous response was the phrase "if it isn't hurting it isn't working" to justify this lunacy.

Inner city riots in Toxteth and Brixton, Handsworth and St Paul's, mass youth unemployment and major industrial confrontations were the outcomes of early Thatcherism.

Following his successful defeat of the steelworkers, Ian McGregor an abrasive and ruthless reducer of headcount with a real antipathy to Trade Unions was appointed Chairman of the National Coal Board. This was to be the final confrontation between the most spirited and militant vanguard of the labour movement, the NUM, and the full power of the state. It was a clash between those who balanced social as well as economic costs against those whose considerations never extended further than balance sheet calculations.

The defeat of the miners in the great strike of 1984 – 1985 reflected the Government's unswerving determination to totally crush the NUM. Thatcher dubbed them "the enemy within" demonising strikers alongside terrorists and the IRA. The government were correct in their strategy that a defeat of the miners would shatter the confidence and resolution of the entire labour movement. The five billion pounds they reputedly spent in mobilising the state was therefore deemed to be money well spent.

The defeat of this strike was the single biggest event to change the entire fabric of British society. It laid a platform for the kind of economy we have today – low skill, low wage, insecure zero-hour contracts, bogus self-employment and unions marginalised. The turbo-capitalism it unleashed had profound effects on the economy, the nature and type of work available and British social attitudes.

As we have outlined the years following Thatcher's election of 1979 saw a dramatic break with cosy consensus politics. The application of monetarism created a new spectre – de-industrialisation.

The first eighteen months saw a loss of over one million manufacturing jobs and for the first time, over a quarter of a million service sector occupations.

As employment levels collapsed, youth unemployment soared, reaching 20% among under 18s by January 1981.

Early in July a series of riots erupted in the inner areas of many of England's major cities. There were nine consecutive nights of rioting, looting and arson in more than 30 towns and cities (Financial Times, 13th July 1981).

Panic ensued, a response was crucial and it came in the form of a massively expanded role for the Manpower Services Commission. It became the key state agency acting to mitigate the political consequences of the return of mass unemployment.

Basically the proposition was that all unemployed 16 year olds would lose their entitlement to supplementary benefit. Instead they were to be offered a place on a new foundation training scheme initially covering 300,000 trainees.

The training, lasting one year, would have three months off-the-job provision, with the remaining nine months work experience with an employer.

THE YOUTH TRAINING SCHEME

A permanent bridge from school to work or gangplank to the dole?

As it evolved the Thatcher government's response to mass youth unemployment went far beyond the limited aims of a temporary transition from school to work. Reading through various MSC and government statements reveals a very ambitious programme aiming at promoting conformity to the new realities of the labour market. As much concerned with changing attitudes as aptitudes. Schools it was asserted were simply not preparing students for the world of work.

"Where the need to achieve results in conformity with defined standards and to do so within fixed time limits calls for different patterns of behaviour." (MSC/TSA 1975)

The whole thrust of this explanation was that because of the inadequacy of the schools, and by definition school leavers, they were out of work. Thereby re-packaging the crisis of an economic system as one of individual failure and negative attitudes.

An internal DES memorandum warned that "If young people drop off the educational production line and cannot find work at all, or work that meets their abilities and expectations, then we are only creating frustration with perhaps disturbing social consequences." (Internal DES Memorandum 1984, page 21)

Chillingly the memorandum concluded, "People must be educated once more to know their place." Working class youth were not only to undergo basic skills training but be re-orientated and re-socialised to be more acceptable to employers. This implied an across the board lowering of youth expectations. David Young on becoming MSC Chairman stated, "Youth rates of pay in Britain are far too high" and "The young should be a source of cheap labour" (Observer, 7th February 1982). Employers were invited to participate in the scheme on the following terms.

"You now have the opportunity to take on young men and women, train them and let them work for you almost entirely at our expense, and then decide whether or not to employ them." (The Director, October 1982).

The content of the training had to reconcile two contrasting objectives. Firstly, employers wanted trainees to carry out specific tasks and be competent in attaining a minimum and acceptable standard in their execution. The concept of "transferrable skills" required competence in a range of tasks applicable to a broad range of occupations. This attempted to address labour market realities by recognising that many trainees would end up working for a series of employers in the new economy. They therefore needed a skillset that enabled them to gain employment over a range of occupations.

The origins of this view leaned heavily on the ideas of F. W. Taylor dubbed the "Father of scientific management". Taylor's ideas were a response to the working environment he faced in the last century and were quickly exploited by major industrialists, notably Henry Ford. Faced with a large and diverse immigrant workforce and varying levels of literacy and language barriers he needed to introduce a system of work organisation that overcame these obstacles.

This involved a two-pronged approach. Firstly a complex engineering and assembly process such as car manufacture was broken down into a series of simple tasks, easily mastered. Secondly work methods were to be strictly analysed using "time and motion techniques" to ensure maximum speed and efficiency. Taylor believed in the principle of "the one best way" to carry out tasks. This "best way" was to be determined by management alone and rigidly enforced to deter any variances.

Taylor believed that the one and only motivator at work was money and therefore payment by results was to be encouraged.

Taylor's view of training in this situation was dismissive. Once simple tasks such as "reading a dial" were mastered "their training is over".

Taylor therefore institutionalised the separation of brain and hand, concept and execution. The former was entirely the preserve of management and the entire system enforced by a rigid command and control ethos.

This view of the economy and industrial organisation was oblivious to developments in the economy instigated virtually exclusively in foreign-owned firms demonstrating astonishing successes where previously failure was endemic.

In "Becoming World Class" Clive Morton outlined how by training and educating the workforce at Komatsu at Birtley in North East England, astonishing levels of quality, productivity and continuous improvement were the norm. A large proportion of the workforce were ex-shipyard workers and miners previously unemployed. By developing their staff they aimed to train them beyond the needs of their immediate job tasks "In order that they would be able to make an even greater contribution to company performance".

When astonished visitors commended "Where do you get labour like this?" the reply was significant. "We fish from the same pond as you, but we treat people differently."

The whole emphasis in YTS on low level basic and transferable skills reflected the views of many in the Tory party whose lack of practical exposure to manufacturing reflected their out-dated approach.

This was graphically stated in the most blunt terms by Conservative Chancellor of the Exchequer Nigel Lawson in 1984. He described Britain's future as "No tech rather than low tech". Some in the Tory party hoped the chronic unemployment and manufacturing meltdown would be offset in the future by the new technological "sunrise industries" and the burgeoning financial services sector. Lawson not only considered this unrealistic but actually arrant nonsense. His vision for future school leavers was that as our economy declined, low-tech jobs may be the only type available. The future for Britain's youth seemed to be as a nation of personal servants, textile sweat shops, "burger flippers" and caterers for tourists in a gigantic heritage theme park.

Today one of the UK's largest employers, Macdonalds represents the epitome of all these trends. Tasks are de-skilled and standardized. Precise cooking times and settings are outlined with even placing burgers on a grill conducted to a rigid procedural sequence. Everything from food preparation to cleaning floors and locking up are standardised in order to conform to and ensure a standard offer of food and service at every outlet. Employment at the time of writing, is dominated by part-time and zero hours contracts. Nigel Lawson was nothing if not visionary.

SCHOOL LEAVERS 1979 – 1986

I left Harold Secondary School in 1974 after three years teaching there. It was with regret, but with the school scheduled to close few assurances were on offer as to what the future held. As it turned out the majority of the staff transferred to the Heneage School barely half a mile away. This was also slated for closure at some time in the future, so the whole demoralising process was to be repeated. This meant that both schools serving the East Marsh were to disappear.

After nearly ten years teaching Economics at the Immingham School, seven miles out of Grimsby I fancied a complete change. Scanning the job market I applied for a job at Grimsby college as Lecturer in Charge of Vocational Preparation. With the majority of school leavers now moving into this area I was interested in getting involved in the training, setting up work experience and ultimately trying to secure jobs.

Although fairly cynical about the government's motives behind this "new deal" for school leavers you rationalise this with what you might achieve at a local level. By a real quirk of fate I returned once again in 1983 to Harold Street which was now re-branded as Grimsby College's Harold Street Annexe.

"IT'S WORK JIM, BUT NOT AS WE KNOW IT" - DAVE WAGSTAFF
1983 – 1987

I interviewed Dave Wagstaff because as well as being a good mate he was instrumental in the running of the Youth Training Scheme at the Harold Street Annexe of Grimsby College.

I began by asking Dave how he got into this sort of work.

"I began in the Careers Office at Grimsby in 1975, I was promoted to manage the Youth Opportunities Programme (the fore-runner of YTS). My job was split geographically between Grimsby and Scunthorpe. Basically my job was to organize the work placement side of the scheme, known as W.E.E.P. (Work Experience on Employers Premises). Scunthorpe offered a far better environment than Grimsby, given that the bulk of placements were at British Steel Scunthorpe. With a background of apprenticeships and on-site trainers they were far more geared up to giving real experience and training and in many cases job outcomes.

"Obviously I was in regular contact with Grimsby College as alongside their in-house programme they also required work experience with local employers. At this point in the evolution of youth training the programme content was heavily orientated to "life skills", interview techniques and CV presentation. In other words the reason for youth unemployment was because young people were not presenting themselves correctly, rather than a shortage of jobs in a collapsing economy.

"About this time, 1982 – 1983 a plethora of "Managing Agents" – private sector trainers, mushroomed in Grimsby. This was in line with MSC's avowed aim to welcome the private sector into youth training and a barely disguised antipathy to more mainstream college and FE providers.

"I was appointed Senior Lecturer in Industrial Liaison for Grimsby college in 1983 when YTS was really taking off. Obviously, I was at an advantage in that I brought almost one hundred employers and contacts from my previous roles. This meant that the Harold Street Annexe was up and running very quickly and we were well placed to offer a viable package to both local employers and school leavers. The main college was big enough and with an extensive portfolio of courses to attract large numbers.

"Like many involved, all my political instincts opposed YTS. It could be critiqued on so many levels – fiddling the unemployment figures, subsidising employers from the public purse and issuing a certificate of experience rather than actual qualifications.

"I balanced this in my own mind that at least at a local level we were trying to address employment issues in the town. It was becoming increasingly difficult for 16-20 year olds to get a start on the employment ladder. We tried to break the adage "that you can't get a job because you've no experience". I also thought at the time that it would act as a base for further training and development and that we might be able to establish a training culture among employers.

"Looking back with the benefit of hindsight I didn't realise how rigidly the MSC would rule the scheme and how downright cynical some employers were. Although it was in everyone's interest to eliminate the bad employers in a way we conspired in the process by encouraging employers to see it as a filter for selection before employing trainees.

"It's difficult to quantify but perhaps 20% of employers could be classed as "bad apples". Many were genuine and wanted to employ young people.

"Walking around the town today I see countless examples of people who got their start on this scheme and are still in the same industry today.

"Down at Harold Street the Multi-Skills Course was by far the biggest. Students would select from a portfolio of courses comprising Fish Processing, Motor Vehicle, Catering, Clerical, Building, Painting and Decorating, Carpentry and Joinery and Hairdressing.

"Initially three options were mandatory before eventually filtering into their chosen career path."

I asked Dave to summarise, thirty odd years on, his verdict on the scheme.

"There was a constant tension. David Young as head of MSC was rigid and radical in a drive to privatise FE. He was about breaking up the FE sector and removing the Industrial Training Boards (ITBs) which he claimed had too much Trade Union input. As the government were desperate to reduce the growing army of unemployed, the scheme was always more about quantity than quality.

"We were trying to do the right thing by school leavers in a shrinking job market. The MSC offered their view of how things should be run and FE's response was weak and fragmented. The MSC was becoming increasingly responsible for the funding of FE and used this leverage to nullify opposition.

"Locally we had a Manager at Harold Street, Paul Bishop, who gave people their head and tried to be as flexible as possible. Locally the

Harold Street Annexe was a major "cash cow" for the college with over 500 trainees on the books.

"There was a serious lack of quality in some locally provided training schemes. This went unchallenged for far too long."

I then asked Dave if he was doing the same job today what differences would he encounter?

"Today it would be a much harder job. Public opinion, the media, and a narrative of "shirkers" have reduced the level of sympathy for the unemployed. This I think would make recruiting employers harder.

"Entry level jobs are not as plentiful today and many, for example fish processing with all the harsh working conditions would I think be less attractive to today's school leavers.

"The whole culture of zero hours contracts, agency working and DWP "work trials" have institutionalised the employer as being "in the driving seat". This would seem to again nullify opportunities for school leavers."

Dave then analysed the whole premise of "choice" for school leavers.

"At entry level jobs you are not really giving people a choice in the widest sense. Careers advice, literally boils down to vacancy advice. The 2,000 or so school leavers in Grimsby have a choice – but that choice is limited to what's on offer in the town. It's all about filling vacancies. Similarly at college you have a choice from what courses are available. At a national level YTS paved the way for what has been dubbed "Socialism for the employing class and capitalism for the rest." For the first time it institutionalised subsidising employers.

It paved the way for mass privatisation, tax credits, housing benefit and many other devices by the state to subsidise the activities of those at the "top of society".

"DRINKING IN THE LAST CHANCE SALOON" - TONY McLERNON

Tony once again figures prominently in this account. This time his story has moved on to the period when he worked closely with me in running the YTS programmes at the Harold Street Annexe of Grimsby College.

I asked Tony to recall those days in a break he was taking from renovating his bungalow out at Holton le Clay.

"I returned to the UK from building out in Germany. The recession in 1981 was unrelenting. One hundred thousand were being added to the dole queues every month. As the unemployment increased skilled workers' wages plummeted. The construction industry is always the bell weather for the economy – always the first into any recession. Profit margins were down from our industry average of between 3% to 6% to less than 2% or even breakeven as firms tried to tough out the general depression.

"I jumped at the chance when I was made a permanent Lecturer in Brickwork and Construction. Just as YTS was coming on line in 1983. We put together an imaginative offer based around a reasonably large list of vocational options. We marketed the programme as the Multi-Skills Course. You could pick three vocational options and use this as a vehicle to select your preferred specialism as the course progressed.

"Looking back, we had 500 students on the programme and they were generally very good, well worth working with. Things were very harsh throughout the district and we tended to recruit from most of the working-class areas of Grimsby, not exclusively the East Marsh.

"The greatest satisfaction I derived from the job was seeing "trainees" gain employment or moving some of the more able onto mainstream craft apprenticeships.

"Both myself and Pete always kept our ears to the ground for new opportunities. Although YTS became increasingly bureaucratic and centrally driven. Further Education has always been a fertile ground for new approaches and innovation.

"Walking around Grimsby Fish Dock we noted that the average age of filleters and fish processors was very high indeed. Many were in their fifties, sixties or even seventies. New blood was not coming into the industry. Parents would advise their kids to steer clear as the total decimation of Grimsby's Deep Water Fleet cast a long gloomy shadow across the docks. Many had left the industry and Agency working was becoming increasingly common, bringing all the insecurity and negativity of the "new labour market".

However, even a cursory examination of the facts revealed all was not lost, it wasn't all doom and gloom. Although there was no Deep Water Fleet there was still a presence in Near and Middle Water Fishing. This was augmented by fish coming in overland and from big container vessels from Iceland, Norway and Holland. Herring and mackerel came in from Scotland. This compensated for the reduced direct landings on the Fish dock. With the health aspects of seafood being shrewdly marketed and the demand for fish bringing buoyant auction prices, things were changing. Grimsby may have lost its huge catching fleet, but it was still a major processing and distribution hub. We were becoming the Billingsgate of the North. You didn't have to be Einstein to realise that there was only one outcome, a big future demand for labour. Labour with the skills to process the volumes and yields required.

"We canvassed over 80 employers, many small with under ten employees to ascertain interest in the proposed scheme. We asked them what skills they needed and designed bespoke programmes to address them. We negotiated with Ken Beeken, Secretary of the Fish Merchants Association and rented a stand, a large chiller, messroom and offices on Grimsby's iconic pontoon. The pontoon was open to all the elements, with filleters working on the dockside, the offices and messrooms being located on overhead gantries.

"We recruited two experienced filleters to train and liaise with employers. The course was extremely popular and although predominantly male dominated, some girls did very well. We had over 60 trainees who were split into three groups on a roll-on, roll-off basis. Our programme covered every aspect of the fish trades. We introduced performance criteria, so for example filleting with timed operations and measured yields to determine competence. This was badged by City & Guilds and for the first time there was a nationally accredited qualification in the industry. The whole course was practical, even the off the job element on the pontoon was run like a working business. Trainees would go to the early morning fish auction, prepare, package and sell the fish. Initially we used cheaper fish like coley and whiting for them to develop their "knife skills" but they soon progressed to "prime fish", haddock and cod.

"We attracted intense publicity in the local press, at last, some good news! We made a promotional video featuring the work they were doing and getting the trainees to talk about their experiences working on the Fish Dock. They were extremely positive even though in the winter months the conditions they worked in were incredibly demanding.

"We had a good number of trainees who came from out of area on a residential basis for short courses in the specific skills we offered. One Hull factory sent ten of their employees for a week to gain new skills and we had some who came up from Lowestoft to specialise in flat fish filleting. The point is we were unique, no one else offered what we could and certainly nobody had the same level of expertise and organisation."

Tony is still involved in training and education today in Grimsby. I asked him for his views on the current system.

"Looking at the apprenticeship system today I have very mixed views. If we look at those occupations that could be described as "craft based" – by that I mean bricklaying, electricians, hairdressing or a chef for example, then I am broadly positive. The training is administered by Skills Agencies representing the relevant industries and vocations and is broadly sound. What I do object to are the incorporation of £2 an hour shelf stackers and trolley organisers that have been co-opted into the system. A wholly cynical attempt to provide cut-price labour and boost numbers to allow the government to claim it has some kind of industrial strategy.

"It trashes the whole concept of an apprenticeship which I believe means acquiring a real skill which enables progression along a career path.

"The other worry I have is that people of my age are the last representatives of those who received a thorough and comprehensive craft apprenticeship. We are now drinking in the last chance saloon. I see Lecturers and instructors who have a much more limited skills base and experience than those of my generation and the quality of instruction is being diluted. We need to tap into the vast knowledge still available, after the collapse of apprenticeships in the seventies, eighties and nineties.

"Brexit of course highlights many other potential issues. Industry should be planning now for a shortage of labour, skilled, semi-skilled and unskilled. They should be training now in preparation for this skills deficit. This will require a massive vocational programme with incentives and support for industry training."

I asked Tony how confident he was in what would seem to be an obvious policy being implemented.

"I'm sorry but I'm increasingly cynical. British short termism and the inability to think strategically seem to dominate all aspects of life today."

PART THREE - WHAT'S TO BE DONE?

SCHOOL LEAVERS ON THE EAST MARSH TODAY.

"The philosophers have only interpreted the world, in various ways. The point, however, is to change it." – Karl Max, Eleven Theses on Feuerbach.

The questions posed by contemporary economists and politicians demonstrate how the current system manifestly fails to deliver for substantial numbers. Why in a country twice as rich as it was even 30 years ago have poverty rates doubled? What economic and social forces have transformed Britain into one of the most unequal and socially fragile countries in the developed world? Is poverty a symptom of personal inadequacies or because of a lack of jobs and opportunities?

Unfortunately, the strong line promoted by first the coalition government and latterly the current Conservative administration is the former. Poverty is almost labelled as a "lifestyle choice" largely self-inflicted. Osborne's attempt to repackage poverty as an ongoing struggle between "strivers" and "shirkers" represents classic divide and rule tactics. Egged on by a partisan media he recounts tales whereby early risers on their way to work are confronted by the drawn curtains of their feather bedded neighbours on social security.

The point I always make when countering this caricature is that when full employment is on offer, the overwhelming majority want to work. Rising poverty and diminished opportunities cannot be explained away as the result of individual failings or inadequacy.

The real cause obviously is found in the great social and economic upheavals of the last thirty years. Today's school leavers face a hardening political environment and a jobs market characterized by the spread of low pay and chronic insecurity.

The neo-liberal argument that allowing the rich to get richer would be to everyone's benefit as wealth "trickles down" has been road tested to destruction. Obviously such a view has suited those at the top very well, hence its continued durability in the face of all the evidence to the contrary. This small group of the economic elite have grabbed an increasingly large share of the cake affecting not just the increasing gaps in income and wealth, but to an expanding divide in life chances. It has spread deprivation, blighted lives and fragmented communities like the East Marsh.

Britain is governed by an economic model that is incapable of delivering decent incomes and life chances to far too many of its citizens. This is not an inevitability, like most things in life it is about a choice. To change an economy that for too many is broken means changing the model rather than blaming the victims.

The alternative model must prioritise the reduction in inequality, enhance opportunities and most importantly enable decent living standards by raising wages and improving job security. It means challenging and reversing the economic choices of the last three decades on how the fruits of growth are shared. Other choices are possible.

The life-changing decision of 1980's Thatcherism to drive Britain down a market-orientated, union-busting deregulation route; its selling off of public housing and rolling privatisation of public services is increasingly under attack. The General Election of 2017 showed huge swathes of the electorate are increasingly disenchanted and Jeremy Corbyn's transformational manifesto created tremendous enthusiasm and voter engagement.

Even capitalism's major exponents see problems with its long-term sustainability. A system condemning 30% of the population to live blighted lives clearly carries huge social, political and economic risks. The substantial and growing imbalance of a model designed around poverty wages and huge corporate and private profits cannot hold indefinitely. Unless the political will is there to reverse the course of the last 30 years capitalism will literally eat itself. As declining wages deliver poorer and poorer markets credit is expanded to fill the gap thus injecting increasing instability and simply providing a smoke screen to economic realities. Realities that mean the periodic crises and slumps so endemic to our system.

Without a radical programme of change to tackle these issues far too many of today's school leavers will be unable to fulfil even their most modest ambitions.

The final section of this story covers those individuals, charities and organisations working on the East Marsh to enhance the environment and provide hope and a sense of direction and purpose for school leavers and their families. Many of their stories are inspirational and they reflect community activism to combat an austerity agenda presiding over the dismantling of the Welfare State and the post-war consensus.

Cameron attempted to camouflage reality with his "Big Society" calling on the charity and voluntary sector to plug the gaps in the public realm and provision. It has produced what J.K. Galbraith highlighted decades ago "Private Affluence and Public Squalor".

However, we may be currently undergoing a paradigm shift, as seismic as that experienced in the 1980s. Jeremy Corbyn in his speech at the Labour Party conference in 2017 described the capitalism of today as a rentier economy. This is light years away from the market economy lionised by Theresa May and Philip Hammond, clearly panic stricken by Corbyn's analysis. The previous means of achieving economic "growth" – stimulating a housing "bubble", extracting profit from public services and the over-arching influence of the financial sector are not the hallmarks of a productive economy. Corbyn accurately described the system as an extractive one seeking rent. This model is highly unstable and is increasingly seen as broken. The undoubted panic among Conservative politicians is that the more astute strategic thinkers can see a definite move away from the beliefs that have so dominated the last forty years.

The change required is a root and branch rebalancing of the economy from rich to poor, from the South East to the rest and from rentier capitalism to a productive system.

Harry Leslie Smith whose life has straddled two centuries has written and spoken extensively about the grinding poverty and injustice of life in Barnsley during the Depression. Unfortunately, he sees growing parallels today in the crises in social housing and the NHS, as Brexit further divides the country.

However, Harry's optimism and resilience remain undimmed. He believes change is not just possible, but that ultimately progressive politics will triumph.

The stakes are high, and the outcome of the current struggle will have a crucial impact on the future direction of society, the economy and the life chances of the upcoming generation especially.

Harry has entitled the mission of his book a "call to arms. It is to be hoped that his sincerity and optimism is not misplaced. The alternatives are chilling and are contained in the warning of the title of his latest book "Don't let my past be your future".

"BROTHER, SISTER LET ME HELP YOU" –
SOCIALISM IN ALL BUT NAME - TERRY ATKINSON
(FRANCISCAN HYMN)

255 WEELSBY STREET

Terry's life story spans every aspect of this book. He attended Harold Street School and left in the late sixties. He started his working life as an apprentice Butcher before taking other career choices. He was taken on as a Technician at Harold Street when supporting the Youth Training Scheme in the 1980s. Finally, he became an Anglican priest whose ministry was St Andrew's Church on the junction of Albion Street and Garibaldi Street next to Freeman Street in the centre of the East Marsh. He furnished me with unique insights spanning the entire period covered in my story.

Terry paints a picture of life in the community in the sixties and early seventies.

"For all the machismo surrounding fishing, hard men leading hard lives, women were the glue that bound both family and community.

With men away at sea for huge periods women were the organisers and the ones who coped. Most men were either employed on the docks or fishing. A definite sub-culture developed to mitigate the hardships and problems this entailed. There were many Danes in the area and Danish customs and eating habits were adopted. We used to get bacon bones and use dried peas to make ham and pea soup. If someone was in trouble or in need women tended to pick it up quickly and support came in every guise. There were three prominent grocers Newmans, Johnsons & Smith and Funstons, also a tiny sweet shop, Pattinsons. They were a vital support mechanism as they all allowed "tick" or credit. This kept families going while the main wage-earner was away for three weeks and sometimes "landed in debt" – if there was a bad trip at sea.

Everybody seemed to have a shed and the majority kept pigeons. My vivid memory was there were only three cars in the vicinity of where I lived.

Whilst a pupil at Harold Street I experienced some transgressers being subject to a very harsh disciplinary regime. Many of the staff on reflection were very dedicated and their influence was instrumental in any success I have achieved in life. I really enjoyed Music and R.E. I remember Jack Hall our Music Teacher saying, "You've a powerful voice lad, use it." The teaching was old-fashioned in some respects. While I was there I had many misgivings but now I count those days as among the happiest days of my life. Frank Walsham, another teacher, still remembered to this day as "Mad Wally" spoke Danish and encouraged me to take it up at night school. We studied at the Danish Mission and Church at Lockhill, now a restaurant.

"I returned to Harold Street in 1980 and remained there for six years. I was employed as a Technician at what was now an annexe of Grimsby college just as the Youth Training Scheme (YTS) was coming on stream.

"It was deja vue in terms of my return, but in a totally different position and regime. It took me a while to understand YTS even though I had been a professional Youth Worker. Many of the "trainees" seemed hopeful they would get something out of the scheme. Some got jobs and some especially those doing painting and Decorating set up their own businesses. Talking to many of them, it was obvious that they faced challenging home lives. It was also a time of personal growth for me although at the time I was not a "political animal". Looking back, it is obvious to me that it was a Tory government's desperation to massage the unemployment figures that was a significant factor. Obviously the hundreds of thousands on government schemes were automatically excluded from the unemployment count.

"The positives I take out of this was a very "collegiate" spirit among the trainees, they generally got on well and stuck together. While many had basic or even low expectations they saw the scheme as moving them forward in the world of work.

"Even with the 1980s' recession many firms were around that simply do not exist now. When I took up the priesthood after working away I returned to Grimsby in 2004. One of the first things I did was to have a walk down to the docks and I took some photographs. The overwhelming feeling I had was of profound sadness. I remembered graphically when I was at Junior School at Weelsby Street, we had a trip down to the docks when it was in full flow as the greatest fishing port in the world.

"I wanted to return to Grimsby as my father was terminally ill. I was interviewed by the Bishop and he said with a smile, "There is a vacancy at St Andrew's". Knowing the area intimately, I knew this would be what is deemed to be a "challenge".

"There were only eleven in the congregation and in the ten years of my ministry it increased to fifty.

I knew that to make any impact this was only half of my job as I saw it. Practical Christianity meant to me working in and with the community. We ran a weekly luncheon club and for many who attended it was their only hot meal of the week. We ran line dancing and ballroom dancing in the parish hall and bingo sessions. The bingo prizes were not cash, but items like washing powder, food, cutlery and things for the home,"

I asked Terry what he thought was his biggest achievement.

"Rekindling faith in people who I believe were not well served by either church or Society. People could identify with me as a former Harold Street boy who had educated himself and returned to work in his community."

I asked him what he thought was on offer in terms of job prospects currently for the young in Grimsby.

"My experience in talking with about fifteen of my nieces and nephews is not encouraging. The girls have tried for permanent employment but to no avail, apart from one who completed a BA and went on to teach. The rest of the girls have had intermittent employment but the advent of zero hours contracts and agency working means they have literally given up to concentrate on raising a family. The jobs they have secured tend to be short-term factory work, cleaning or in catering but nothing has turned out to be permanent. The boys have managed to earn a living out of the residue left on the docks, filleting and fish processing.

"Looking back, it's not nostalgia it's the overwhelming feeling of frustration at the way things have declined. Just a waste of economic and human potential. The "Energy Estuary" and wind technology may be a partial answer, but the jury is out.

In my Ministry you need to keep working on your own personal positivity, as despair generates apathy amid the maze of bureaucratic obstacles placed in the way by government departments and agencies.

"Theologically speaking, we are looking at the words "hope" which links in with the future and "honesty". Any government needs to move on from platitudes to positive actions that will enable young people to become earners and provide for their families like their forbears."

At the end of our talk, Terry asked me if I had religious belief. I replied, "No, but I am a socialist."

"Then you are halfway there", he replied with a smile.

"IN THE GARDEN" – ERNIE BROWN
(VAN MORRISON, 1986)

22A GRAFTON STREET

Ernie Brown is Garden Manager and Activities Co-Ordinator at the Oasis Garden Project which is run in conjunction with a host of other activities by the Grimsby Neighbourhood Church. The Church and the Garden and offices are based on Wellington Street virtually at the centre of the East Marsh.

The garden which has won numerous awards, has been transformed from what was formerly a builder's yard and thereafter a dump for supermarket trolleys, fridges and mattresses to a thing of real beauty.

I personally became involved as a volunteer in the garden three years ago. While I am no "Capability Brown" I tend to get involved in the heavier aspects of gardening such as composting and pavement laying.

Ernie manages the vast amount of work required by organising volunteers from all walks of life. If you were composing a CV of desirable qualities for this role, he would tick all the boxes. Gregarious and outgoing he puts people at ease, he has endless patience and a wicked sense of humour.

I asked him what contribution the organisation in general and the garden in particular made to improving the life of the area's residents.

I started by asking Ernie what was the purpose of the garden.

"The garden is a means to an end. We use it as a medium to help people gain self-esteem, build confidence and give them a sense of self-belief in their own ability.

"Basically we produce plants from seeds and cuttings costing virtually nothing. This gives a real sense of achievement to those involved because they see an end product of their labour. Furthermore, we generate substantial and growing sales to the public which is ploughed back into the organisation.

"Our group of volunteers are a varied bunch compromising adults of all ages and abilities. Retired people who want to give something back to the community, and those who may not be capable of getting a job but want to make a contribution. The work is all about talking and socializing and for many becomes a very meaningful highlight of their work."

With a background in catering prior to horticulture, Ernie also runs cookery classes. These show how to produce cheap, healthy and nourishing food often using vegetables grown in the garden.

He also runs a Thursday afternoon walking group, and as a keen student of local history, can explain and discuss various landmarks in the town. Once again though, this is seen as a means to achieve other goals.

"It's not as if we're sat in a circle looking at each other. Because we are walking side by side we do not always have eye contact. People who may be reserved or introverted do not feel intimidated, they can talk more openly about what is important in their lives.

"Yesterday one of our lady volunteers had suffered a bereavement and was upset. We sat her down and tried to console her. Then we got her working in the poly-tunnel alongside someone else and gradually her spirits lifted.

"We're a family here. If someone is upset we deal with it straight away. I often think what we do is a drop in the ocean, but the ocean is made up of lots of drops – that's our philosophy.

"in May this year we had 470 people involved as volunteers or visitors. We get lots of school groups coming in. Kids who came when they were seven and eight are now fourteen, fifteen and sixteen. I am nothing if not enthusiastic. It is important that they see a positive role model – too many lack this at home."

Ernie lives on the East marsh, his verdict on the area is far from black and white.

"I believe the East Marsh is in a process of terminal decline, albeit a slow one. Drugs are a massive problem especially the new Psycho-Active drugs. They are increasingly more powerful and produce some horrendous side effects. Locals refer to users of these new drugs as "Spice Monkeys". This has produced an epidemic of low level acquisitive crime. This by its nature takes place within the community and is often committed in order to obtain short-term goals for drug money.

"The irony is that many of my neighbours are in work although inevitably it is either low paid, insecure or part-time.

"there are many community groups and individuals who make great efforts to improve the community. Without them the future would look very bleak indeed.

"I made a conscious decision to buy a house on the East Marsh. The prime reason boils down to affordability. I actually love living in the area. It all really boils down to your neighbours. I have always baked bread regularly and usually give most of it away to friends and neighbours. I did this when I moved in and this has been a great ice-breaker. This has been reciprocated with fish, crabs and lobsters. I have always been very outgoing and now know dozens in the neighbourhood. We all speak but it has not been achieved without making an effort. Someone with a more reserved or introverted character may have felt more isolated. However, it has worked for me and I have no regrets whatsoever."

"MANY RIVERS TO CROSS" – WENDY JACKSON
(JIMMY CLIFF, 1968)

PRINCIPAL, HAVELOCK ACADEMY, GRIMSBY

David Cameron as Prime Minister famously extolled the virtues of his alma mater, Eton. Describing it as a fine school, he said he wanted everyone to be able to benefit from the kind of life chances and education he had enjoyed. However, when a third of all wealth is inherited, wealth and the opportunities that go with it stays where it is. If a government then actively pursues policies which further accentuate inequalities – closing Sure Start Centres, abandoning Education Maintenance allowances, reducing school and F.E. budgets, then this pronouncement by Cameron is shameless.

Alan Milburn, Chair of the Social Mobility Commission, made two major points. Opportunity is closely related to household income and children's school performance remains tied to their background.

It is against these objective realities that the Principal and staff of Havelock School challenge and struggle with every working day of their lives. Yet, Havelock, in spite of this, is a good school doing an excellent job. The acid test of what is a good school is "would you be happy for your child to go there?" After a very frank and sometimes inspirational interview with the school's Principal I would have to answer unreservedly "Yes".

Wendy, who has worked at Havelock for 19 years, is not your everyday sort of Principal.

"My Dad was a fisherman. I left school at 16 and went on a YTS Scheme. I didn't think about university until I was 30."

However, Wendy's unconventional route to the top has given her a greater understanding of, and a burning desire to improve the community her school serves.

"Virtually everyone in this school comes from the East Marsh. One of our problems is pupil stability. For example, in Year 11 we started out with 200 in the year group and are now down to 136. Evictions, moving to avoid landlords and family breakdown have contributed to the highest mobility rate in the authority. In spite of this our attendance is excellent at 96%. High neighbourhood turnover means community breakdown and cohesion is threatened by drugs, alcohol and domestic abuse.

"When I first started at this school in 1999 this was a failing school. We had 400 on roll (today it is 1,111 and oversubscribed), and only 8% of pupils gained 5 GCSEs; today it is 57%. 52% of our children have free school meals. The number eligible is actually higher but some are too proud to claim. Poverty and unemployment is definitely worsening. A relative watched a series of drug deals being done from a phone box in the East Marsh, with a steady stream of customers throughout. This is an environment which is all too common to many of our pupils.

"But the question I pose is "How do we have such fantastic kids when often their home life is chaotic?" My answer is that we need to put them in a different environment – restoring order, hope and ambition. We are driven to make sure that every pupil is the best they can be."

As an aside, Wendy vindicated her school's very strong uniform policy.

"We don't want kids who can ill afford it to be competing on designer labels and certain types of trainers. We eradicate this by insisting on no deviation from uniform policy. We don't want distractions, we want concentration on achieving high standards.

"We have a policy of free school breakfasts for all pupils – the costs are significant but the benefits of starting the day right are substantial. We open at 8 a.m. although many arrive well before then. We start learning at 8.20 a.m. If required we'll buy shoes or trousers, its all part of making their lives as pleasant and productive as we can so we try to minimise barriers to achievement.

"We are now over-subscribed. We're committed to improving the life chances. We want to give them choices, not be doomed to unemployment. We want them to go away and fulfil themselves educationally, but ideally return to their own community and give something back."

I asked Wendy if she thought there was an over-emphasis on an academic curriculum, which was actually short-sighted and unsuited to a proportion of her intake. I cited the massive skill shortages in construction, engineering and other disciplines.

"We recognise this and have introduced Hair and Beauty, Hospitality and Catering, health and Social Care and Sports and Leisure qualifications. We have also introduced some basic qualifications in Information Technology, a Work Skills qualification and Adult Literacy and Numeracy examinations."

I asked Wendy if all staff have bought in to what seems to be an all-consuming job.

"Most have bought in, although for some it is not for them. The pastoral care at this school has always been great, but the systems to ensure qualifications and job outcomes were clearly under-developed.

"The East Marsh is within the top twenty most deprived wards in the UK. Grimsby has the highest number of N.E.E.T.s (Not in Employment, Education or Training) in the country. More and more of our students are bucking this trend going either into our sixth form, Grimsby or Frandlin College or Apprenticeships.

"We need to broaden horizons and allow our children access to and information on career paths. We have majored on having dedicated staff to give careers advice and also we have a monthly Business Banquet. This entails local companies coming in and talking about what their plans are and who they are looking to recruit, and the qualifications and training required. We want our kids to access these opportunities. However, the strong message is if you want this sort of employment you will need to put the hours in, do the training, gain the qualifications and embark on lifelong learning. The unskilled and semi-skilled jobs are diminishing and in today's world hardly provide financial stability.

"This school has doubled in size and the numbers going into higher and further education and apprenticeships has increased by 80% in ten years. However I would go further. The situation at present is too loose. I would not allow 16 year olds to leave school, allowing them to carry on their education to 18 and only being signed off if there is a clear career route in place.

"Being part of the David Ross Trust has enriched our offer. Laurence Dellagio, Sebastian Coe, Steve Redgrave and Rebecca Adlington have all come to our school. Their life stores have been inspirational and the confidence and motivation they exude has rubbed off in the classroom.

"But we're only going to go further if we can increase parental involvement in what we are trying to achieve. We are launching a "Community Engagement and Voluntary Programme to invite contributions from parents in supporting any aspects of what we do. This we envisage as a two-way street. If they wish to do any courses from basic literacy and numeracy or GCSE English or Maths then we will help. If they want to use our facilities, for example the library, then we need to offer this resource."

As I walked down the drive from the school entrance in the late September afternoon sunshine, I felt a surge of optimism.

"WE NEED TO BE KNOWN FOR WHAT WE COULD BECOME" - DAVE LAISTER
BUSINESS EDITOR, GRIMSBY & SCUNTHORPE EVENING
TELEGRAPH

I interviewed Dave to ascertain his views on the current state of the Grimsby economy and what prospects there were for school leavers. Dave is well-placed to give a considered verdict as a local lad who has been in the area all his life.

He opened by mentioning one of Grimsby's major issues. "The retention of talent is a big problem. People leave to go to university and all too often do not return. The only way to combat this is to massively increase the volume of graduate level employment opportunities. A very difficult task."

Our conversation turned to Green Energy and the Renewables Industry and the whole concept of the Humber becoming the UK's Energy Estuary. Once again Dave's analysis proved that there will need to be a great deal of energy and imagination employed to ensure the area maximises the potential benefits.

"The local population needs to be upskilled in order to take advantage of the new opportunities. Obviously most of the jobs on this side of the Humber will be in servicing, maintenance and shipping. There is no doubt jobs will be generated and the inshore jobs one would hope would go to locals. The big problem is with the off-shore jobs. Because of shift patterns, say a fortnight on and off, people do not need to live in the area and can quite easily commute. Many large construction projects in the area have seen little benefit in terms of local employment. Indeed, if you shut your eyes in some of the pubs and clubs of Grimsby and Cleethorpes you would think you were in Newcastle or Middlesbrough due to the influx of contractors.

This represents a massive challenge to the area. We need to up our game in terms of leisure and infrastructure to increase the attractiveness of the area and make this an environment that people want to locate to. This is a formidable task, we need to get away from the "Used to be" – "used to be the worlds' greatest fishing port". It's like an albatross around our neck, we need to be known for what we could become. There is a great deal going for us. The industry builds on some of the skills retained in our maritime legacy and in this instance geography is in our favour. We are the last great estuary to be developed fully and are adjacent to the new wind farms.

"There have been estimates of 8,000 jobs generated." I asked Dave how this figure had been arrived at.

"The rule of thumb was that for each turbine a job is created. However, as the technology has become more sophisticated and the turbines are bigger, clearly you need less of them. I estimate that around 2,000 jobs are achievable. However, if we were to get volume manufacturing here as in Hull then things could really take off."

We then turned to the more traditional sectors of the economy. I asked Dave to give me his verdict on their strengths and weaknesses.

"In terms of weaknesses, we are certainly over-reliant on the sea food sector. The industry tends to be low paid and dominated by Agency and part-time working. 30% of the labour force is European migrant labour. If we get a poor deal on Brexit the consequences for the town could be significant. There could be a move to offshore production, leaving Grimsby as a distribution and cold storage hub rather than a centre of processing. However, our area is the only one in the UK to buck the trend of a loss of jobs in the sector, with big hitters like Morrisons coming into the area and making it the centre of their fish processing operation

"Another example of the advantages of a cluster or concentration of seafood producers and food companies in the town is choice. By that I mean some of the giant supermarkets are extremely hard taskmasters and can withdraw a contract to supply them. This contract may not actually leave the town if it is simply taken over by another local firm. Globalisation and transnational ownership also means if hard decisions on investment or indeed reduction or closure are required Grimsby is just another pawn in the game."

We then turned to the Humber Bank Petro-Chemical complex.

"We have two oil refineries that are over fifty years old. Oil is a finite resource and today its future is less assured. We also have the flags of the globe flying on today's Humber Bank – Switzerland, Austria, France and America are all represented. Once again, investment decisions and future policy are decided globally rather than locally."

We then turned to the strengths in the local economy. "The ports and logistics sector is very strong. With the massive congestion on ports and roads in the south the northern ports could reap a huge dividend from a transfer of business from south to north. We are also well-placed to benefit from any positives emerging out of Brexit."

I then turned to the question of the future for school leavers. I asked Dave what advice he would give them.

"I would advise school leavers to look seriously at mechanical and electrical engineering in order that they are multi-skilled and could adapt to a variety of the new opportunities. We need to raise aspirations and move from grand plans and rhetoric to some concrete outcomes to give the young something to aim for.

"If I look back ten years, the future looks brighter. Unemployment is down and the new jobs have arrested the spiral of decline. The town now has a greater sense of purpose and expectation that has been a long time coming."

"THE KETTLE'S ALWAYS ON AND THE DOOR'S ALWAYS OPEN" - CHRIS TAYLOR

PROJECT MANAGER, "YOUR PLACE" – ELIM PENTECOSTAL CHURCH

"As a Minister's wife I was used to moving. The policy then was that you moved every two years. Twenty-six years ago, we were asked to go to Grimsby. We had to get the map out to find out its location. The Elim Mission was an incredibly old building based in Tunnard Street. It is now a boxing club. Nevertheless the congregation was reasonably large with an attendance of 50 – 60 spanning the entire age group. We realised that a massive amount of money would be needed to modernise the building which at that time we just didn't have. We moved to Strand Infants School in Albion Street and then later Weelsby Street Primary School to hold our meetings.

"On the face of it things looked reasonably healthy, but we felt that we were capable of so much more. We needed to be less insular and inwardly focussed and switch to being more community based.

"A defining moment for us was when we all linked hands and formed a circle for a prayer. Alan, my husband then asked us all to turn around and face outwards. Through the windows all around us we could see the cramped streets of terrace houses of Grimsby's East Marsh. We needed to physically become a "church without walls".

For someone new to this approach, Chris has rarely put a foot wrong.

"We took ten people from our own congregation and put them on a course at Grimsby college on how to design surveys, ask the right questions and hopefully get an accurate assessment of community needs. Rather than second guess or impose our own conclusions we wanted to work with the community to implement their wishes and stated needs."

I asked Chris what sort of a reaction all this received.

"As soon as we said we were from the Church barriers went up. We had to deal with a great deal of suspicion and negativity. The breakthrough came when for the first time in my life I had to bid for funding and do a presentation for a Community Pilot Project. I had to go in front of a panel of community representatives and members of the Council. To my genuine surprise and delight we secured a grant of £10,000.

"Now we were really on the move. We bought a former ceramic workshop on Wellington Street and set about renovating it. I had been reading that almost 90% of the prison population was functionally illiterate and innumerate. We began to work with the Probation Service which ex-offenders delivering appropriate courses. We received great support from Grimsby College. An added bonus was that those on probation looking to develop their craft skills carried out extensive renovation. The work completed was to a very high standard. The yardstick for the success of the programme and the environment we try to create is that many continue to come even after their statutory period of probation has ended.

"We have broadened our community offer. We have a marvellous "Oasis" community garden and a host of creative, social and educational activities. The door is always open and the kettle is always on. We never have a cut off on any programme, people can come as long as they want to. As well as our full-time staff we have a large pool of volunteers drawing on a range of experience and abilities. We have a photo gallery of every volunteer and the display is referred to as our "Family Photos". This is the environment we have worked to create, everyone mixing in catering for all age groups and backgrounds."

I asked Chris to summarise her main achievements in what is today an extremely impressive set up.

Apart from establishing attractive and well-maintained facilities that the community can use and take pride in, I think we have changed lives. We have welcomed everyone. Some have been vulnerable and isolated, and we have given them back a sense of belonging.

"It may sound trite but the maxim "the most important person in the world is the one who has just walked in" is our guiding principle. It only takes people about 30 seconds for people to decide if they will come back.

"Organisations have come into the area with big promises, secured funding and failed to deliver. Nobody really thought we would last but we now have a good reputation and community acceptance. We have torn down barriers.

"When I first started applying for funding, I sought advice. Two things stick in my mind. Henry Jesma, vicar of St Aiden's advised, "Never change a project to suit the funding – change the funding to suit the project. Don't just chase the money – be clear about your aims and objectives and mission and stick to them."

"Secondly, it takes twenty years to turn a community around."

Chris summarised, "The other night I was talking with my husband and we realised we will never complete our work here. We have stood on others shoulders and in the future, they will stand on ours.

"We will always rely on external funding, but we are trying to broaden our base to local businesses to continue supporting the community and giving something back.

"The people on the East Marsh have been great, I wouldn't change what I do for the world."

"A WORKING CLASS HERO IS SOMETHING TO BE" – LEE STEPHENS
(JOHN LENNON, 1970)

About three years ago I was contacted by Lee Stephens, the Education Officer at Grimsby Town Football Club. I have known Lee for years due to our involvement in local rugby and football and also as a former work colleague at Grimsby College.

He said he wanted some help and advice about a problem they were having and thought I might be able to help. Intrigued, I went down to the club where we were joined by Graham Rodger, a former player who is now the Community Officer for their vibrant Football in the Community Programme.

I cannot be as frank here as I would wish as the case which is currently going through court proceedings involved a company which is now in liquidation and offered football-based apprenticeships with predominantly non-league clubs. Reporting restrictions have currently been lifted and it is now highlighted regularly in F.E. news. Basically, it involved a labyrinth of subterfuge and alleged falsifying of information in order to gain funding from the F.E. sector for giving training which it is claimed was not delivered. Huge amounts of money were involved but the upshot of all of this was that half of the 20 lads on an NVQ for Sports and Recreation had not received any wages at all.

I drafted letters to one of the colleges involved in an attempt to break the deadlock. Grimsby Town Football Club, Lee Stephens and Graham Rodger are the only people who emerge with any credit from this sorry state of affairs. All their efforts were directed at trying to secure what had been denied to half of the lads on their scheme.

On any given night in the Grimsby Evening Telegraph there are constant reports of crime, vandalism and community breakdown on the East Marsh. I tell the conclusion to the above story, an ending that I am convinced will surprise many people.

A few weeks after I phoned Lee to check on ongoing developments, he updated me.

"We got all the kids in the meeting room and explained the situation to them. Half had been paid the £90 a week training allowance from one college but the other half, who were registered with a different college had still received nothing. We explained we were still working on this but at the moment there was nothing concrete on the table. Most of the lads on the scheme were off the East Marsh and we appreciated apart from the basic injustice of this it was causing real hardship. We thought that was that, and were looking to terminate the meeting. One lad at the back said, "What if we pooled the money so we all got £45 each?" I said, "That's not down to me, I can't make a decision like that". He replied, "What if we take a vote on it?" I agreed and asked for a show of hands in support of his proposal. I have to say it was a memorable moment for me as all 20 hands went up in unison.

This is an example of real solidarity. We never once suggested to the lads any alternatives, we simply presented them with the facts as they stood. It is to their abiding credit that they rejected the notion of self-interest and instead chose to support each other.

"LET'S WORK TOGETHER" – JOHN ELLIS
(CANNED HEAT, 1970)

I returned to interview John for the final part of the book as he has been such an integral driving force in the East Marsh for almost fifty years. He articulated a very clear and well thought out strategy to tackle the problems faced by the community.

Prior to the interview he took me on a tour of The Shalom Youth Club's premises. They were large, airy and very well maintained, with games and leisure areas and a well-planned Sports Hall.

He began by outlining what he sees as the downside of current policy.

"What we desperately need is a multi-agency approach to the East Marsh. At present there is a lot of activity, but it amounts to everyone, including the Council doing little bits and pieces. I have seen at first-hand what can be achieved to completely transform a community."

When I asked John to flesh this out, he mentioned an American example.

"I spent time in Chicago at the Lawndale Community Church. Ironically the Church is sited in a former car showroom where Al Capone bought his limousines – it is still a bit of a tourist attraction for gangster buffs. At the Church they employ ten doctors, an optician and a dentist. The whole area is situated in downtown Chicago and was formerly plagued by drug dealing, crack houses and crime. The system employed by the Church is what they call "sweating equity". It works as follows. When a house in the neighbourhood becomes vacant they buy it up to prevent further deterioration. They then get a young couple who need a house and use their own building team to carry out any structural renovations. The couple then do the basic painting and decorating to bring it up to scratch. Eventually, as this is no instant fix more and more houses enter the scheme and the domino effect is a transformation of the housing stock and a total change in the character of the community. The payoff was incredible, the street we stayed in, and indeed the whole locality was completely free of drugs. I wish this could be replicated over here. However, most of the vacant properties here go to auction. The other major difference is the community. In Chicago the community was predominantly black and they were well-organised and proactive. I think it is a legacy of the Civil Rights movement and of course Obama cut his teeth as a Community Organiser on Chicago's South Side."

John then outlined what he called "simple improvements". Street lighting is poor and needs to be upgraded. There needs to be more pedestrianised areas so that the streets are more community based rather than an artery for cars.

"The upgrade of Victor Street has been an excellent example. The facades have been rendered and new doors and windows installed. The whole street looks much more attractive and the upgrade still looks good three or four years down the line."

John then outlined a vision he has held now for almost all of his tenure in Grimsby.

"What is needed more than anything else is a small community secondary school. When Harold Street School closed and when Heneage School followed, there was no secondary school left to serve the East Marsh."

I interrupted John and told him about my interview at Havelock School and how impressed I was with the way they were trying to give kids from the area the best start they could.

"What we need is a new Harold Street. We need to bring education back into the community. The school would be a visual symbol of investment in the area's young people. I would envisage it as a more practically-based curriculum and in the light of what you have told me a possible annexe to the main Havelock School.

"Finally, we need to keep Shalom open, this is absolutely crucial. This is the last youth centre in North East Lincolnshire. I believe the work of Shalom has stopped the development of gang culture in the area. We categorise young people at risk on a one to five basis. Category one are addicted to risk behaviour – this group will be most at risk to gang culture. Categories 2 – experimenting with risk behaviours. 3 – exhibiting high risk factors and 4 exhibiting low risk factors but will cluster and gravitate to gang behaviours without a programme of support to continually challenge and break down the link with gang culture. The first category – not at risk in these terms means that we target and work with target groups 1 – 4. If the community loses touch with young people then they retreat into a fantasy world divorced from adults and then gang culture develops. I fear this is the future in other disadvantaged local communities such as the Grange and Nunsthorpe that do not have access geographically to the support we offer here."

Finally, I include an extract from the Shalom Youth Project Annual Report for 2016 – 2017. Here John makes a spirited and articulate case for the Shalom approach to youth work. It is absolutely vital that this resource is never lost to this community. It needs to be nurtured, supported and extended. The outcomes are changed lives, life enhancing and a life changing experience. The East Marsh has had some hard knocks in the last forty years, but they are a very lucky community to have John and his team in their corner.

"DEFENDING YOUTH WORK" – JOHN ELLIS

I was standing outside the Centre one Friday evening just after we opened. A white van pulled up and, as I thought initially, two police officers got out. As they got closer to my amazement one of the occupants turned out to be a Youth Worker resplendent in a yellow jacket. He explained he was on a joint patrol with the police. My comment was "This is the death of youth work". He replied that it was 'positive engagement'! Positive engagement for whom, I wondered.

In his paper 'Youth Work: A Manifesto for Our Times' Bernard Davies asks 'has youth work ever been so fashionable – or at greater risk?' He continues 'All over the country services which in the past could barely give it (youth work) time of day have suddenly discovered that it can reach previously (for them) unreached and unreachable parts of the adolescent population.

Davies concedes that 'this new youth work chic is very flattering' Youth Work appears to have come in from the cold. 'Partnership' is the new buzz word. We are urged to adopt an 'integrated approach'. This all seems fine. But all is far from well and the

214

cracks are beginning to appear. The fundamental problem is that our new-found allies are attracted to Youth Work's product but have little understanding of, or patience with, the process. Because the process leads to the product – no process, no product – we may well find that our integrated mates give up, leaving youth work more isolated than ever.

All this, of course, is on the back of the present moral panic about 'anti-social behaviour'. Attend any community group and much of the agenda will be taken up with problems with the 'yufe'. It only ranks just below 'dog fouling' in the horrors addressed by the worthy residents who all appear to be politically a little to the right of Genghis Khan! A couple of years ago Safer communities produced a list of 'community concerns' containing a lengthy catalogue of crimes – in the middle of which appeared 'groups of young people'. Keith Towler, a Children's Commissioner, stated in The Times, 'The ASBO legislation has made the public think that hanging around and chatting on street corners was now illegal, he said "it seems we now disapprove of normal childhood behaviour. Hanging around, kicking a ball around and chatting and laughing **is** normal, but people think the police should be called to deal with it. It is into this bizarre muddle that youth work has unwittingly been drawn and it is an unholy alliance we will live to regret!

The PR problem that Youth Work has always suffered from is that the process is a lengthy one taking place over years rather than days or weeks. Take a snapshot at any point along the process and nothing appears to be happening at all and the only explanation those outside the process can adduce is 'that at least it keeps them off the streets'.

What then is this much misunderstood process? It has a number of absolutely vital elements. Remove any one and the whole process grinds to a halt.

1) In the first place it is about the voluntary association of workers and young people. Young people don't have to be there – they choose to be there. As soon as youth work moves an inch from this voluntary basis the process is compromised.

2) Then the setting is a leisure one. The young people are associating freely in their leisure time – enjoyment and fun lie at the heart of the process. It follows from this that young people are in a position of power which they will experience in few other settings. In purely negative terms they vote with their feet, but in a positive sense they are in control of th depth of their involvement. In the midst of all this apparently chaotic activity something very subtle happens. Like the delicate strands of a web a relationship of trust and understanding builds between worker and young person and that is the key to the whole process. Like all relationships it takes time, it cannot be forced or prescribed.

It is extremely fragile, at least in the initial stages. In the interaction between worker and young person, however, it becomes increasingly robust. Oddly enough it frequently develops through conflict situations. This is why agreeing and holding boundaries is central to the whole process.

So, an outsider visiting a youth work setting would be at a loss to grasp what was going on. Nobody seems to be 'doing' anything. But great skill is required to develop a relationship with young people and the more dysfunctional the young person, the greater skill required. It is this ability to reach young people on the margins that has attracted other services. It is these young people who are in the eye of the storm so far as anti-social behaviour is concerned. But the apparent ease with which a skilled worker can build relationships with seemingly unreachable young people is deceptive and leads those who have other agendas to think that the process can be used in short-term, target-driven work that seeks to 'turn young people around' and it cannot.

The reason this work is particularly effective with dysfunctional young people is quite simply that it is meeting the most significant need in their lives – a long term sustained relationship with an adult that holds even when the wheels fall off. The question posed by The Beatles is still a relevant one – 'What would you do if I sang out of tune, would you stand up and walk out on me?'

3) The process is holistic and non-judgemental. It treats the young person as an integrated human being – not a collection of 'issues' that require to be fixed. The drift in youth work away from this holistic approach is alarming. Youth Workers are actually heard talking about triaging young people as if they were running some kind of A & E Department. Perfectly normal activities that any young person might expect to simply enjoy are now justified as 'diversionary activities' and bizarre statistics adduced to show that ASB has been reduced thereby. Young people – and their parents – need to protest at the notion that if they were not engaged in these activities they would be creating mayhem in the community! The reason why it is only a holistic approach that is effective is that young people are not like toasters. If your toaster breaks down you can take it apart and repair it … if you try the same approach with your poorly cat …! Young people often struggle with problems but these problems are not broken bits that can be fixed. They are a complex weave of social and psychological factors that can only be tackled in the context of the whole person. Any other approach is doomed to failure.

4) The process seeks to take young people beyond their present horizons. In the first place it provides a safe and secure environment where young people can try out new

things and develop new skills. They receive praise and recognition for their efforts and are encouraged to take responsibility for themselves and their actions. For high risk young people this may be the only setting in which they can experience these positives in a world where toxic relationships are the norm. It never ceases to amaze how exposure to a positive secure environment, for even a couple of hours a week, begins to work its magic and counteract so much that is negative and toxic.

At Shalom we have applied this process consistently for over forty years in one of the UK's most deprived communities. Nearly 4,000 young people have been beneficiaries and so many can bear witness to this being a life-enhancing, life-changing experience. We know the process works and we are passionate about defending it and securing it for the young people who deserve better from the community than to be regarded as the end of civilisation!

John W. Ellis
Project Manager
Shalom Youth Project

"GRIMSBY, PAST ITS GLORY DAYS BUT STILL HOPING" - GABY HINSLIFF

6TH MARCH 2015 – GUARDIAN

Gaby arrived in Grimsby prior to the 2015 General Election and wrote an article for the Guardian newspaper. She was analysing whether the Labour vote was vulnerable to a UKIP fantasy world of excluded foreigners and a reconstituted fishing fleet.

The power of Gaby's article stemmed from her intimate knowledge of the town. Prior to moving on to national journalism she was a cub reporter on the Grimsby Evening Telegraph. When I read her article, it was interesting to compare her views with my own and the many people I have interviewed. Given the scale and timeframe of the period covered they are remarkably similar.

Gaby used to work at the Grimsby Evening Telegraph offices at Riby Square at the bottom end of Freeman Street. From the upstairs offices you would have a panoramic view of the Dock offices, the Dock Tower and the entrance to Fish Dock Road. Interspersed among some of these iconic buildings are serious signs of neglect and decay, crumbling buildings and sterile wasteland.

She begins, "Stand on the corner of the building I once worked and the past is right there, crumbling in front of your eyes. On the one side, abandoned warehouses on the fringe of the old dock, seagulls swooping through gaping roofs. On the other steel shuttered empty shops and the top of Freeman Street, once the roaring heart of the town. In the 1970s, it was pay day every day when the fishing boats came in, a pub every few steps and still men queuing out of doors. But you can dwell here with the ghosts or do what I did last week and walk into Grimsby's present."

Gaby looks at the docks today and sees giant cranes emptying the bellies of ships and the haul glistens in the morning sun – not fish but cars, imported, half a million of them. Offshore she sees the whirring blades of the windfarms. Renewable energy is the new big hope for jobs.

"In a town where hopes get dashed too often." Gaby moves on to the many problems of a town exposed to economic shock.

"I could write about stories of factories shedding locals and hiring foreigners on lower wages … I could write about old men drinking on street corners before 10 a.m. and absent buy to let landlords snapping up family homes, splitting them up and renting rooms to all-comers, letting streets slump into disrepair; about poverty sharpening resentment of anyone getting something for nothing."

But Gaby highlights other truths. Like the neighbour who sent around her daughter with some of whatever she was cooking for dinner because "Mam's far away" – in an area where everyone else's mam lived just around the corner.

She observes shoppers and staff in the precinct, "Everyone talks to each other. Nobody's buying much but they're not lonely either."

She remembers the night life of her youth, "I'm reminded of Saturday nights when everyone knew everyone, a whole town half drunk and up for it, queueing in the salty wind for the nightclub on Cleethorpes Pier."

She quotes Grimsby's Labour MP, Melanie Onn saying, "She can't remember when unemployment wasn't an issue."

With the final demise of fishing in the seventies, Grimsby made a spirited attempt to rebrand itself as "Food Town", diversifying into food processing. Again, this relaunch has not been without its difficulties. The two factories dominating the industry at the end of the 1980s were Findus and Birds Eye. Findus closed in the early 1990s with the loss of over 900 jobs, and Birds Eye followed in 2006 with closure and 600 redundancies.

Gaby clearly retains a great deal of affection for the town where she spent the formative years of her career. She has however worries and misgivings about the future.

Grimsby's latest stab at reinvention is at the heart of the "Energy Estuary" and renewables. What if this resurgence is patchy and the jobs don't materialize in the volumes being promised?

"Then there's only so many times hope can wash in and out on the tide before it's gone for good."

"ALL THE WAY" – MICHAELA KEETLEY
(FRANK SINATRA, 1957)
ASSISTANT MANAGER, SHALOM YOUTH PROJECT

I interviewed Michaela in John Ellis's office at the Shalom. She is a great example of what this organisation has achieved and what it has given people. Now Michaela is using this in her work and making a huge contribution to the community she grew up in.

Michaela talked about her early life.

"I was brought up in Rutland Street and did not have the easiest of starts. My Mum was a very hard working, loving mum who juggled about four cleaning jobs interspersed with cash in hand working on the land. My Dad was a fisherman who liked a drink.

"I first came to Shalom when I was five in 1977, I am number 534 on the membership board. By the time I was 13, I was spending a great deal of time here. It is difficult to explain unless you have been a part of Shalom how important this place is and how the people who work here are so vital in supporting you and the life choices you make. At first, this was just a place where I socialised with my friends, it's only later that you realise what a difference it makes to your life.

"Although I had things to do at home to help my mum, I didn't like school and effectively left at 13. I was working at Seasparkle on Grimsby dock by the time I was 14 packing prawns – cash in hand.

"When I was 18 I had a baby boy and by the time I was 22 I was the mum of three and I loved every minute of it. I had something to love and three kids that loved and needed me. I was determined to give my children a better life than I had.

"I brought my kids to the Mother and Toddler Group at Shalom. They were all baptized at the Church and my life settled down on a more even keel. This was shattered when my little girl was taken ill and was found at three years of age to have a hole in the heart and defective valves.   She was taken to Leeds hospital and I felt desperate and alone. John Ellis walked into the hospital and he will never know what his support meant to me.

"As my kids grew up, I had more time to myself and I started to think a great deal about how people lived and struggled in this community. I wanted to help. I wanted to give the same kind of support at Shalom that had been given to me.   I started to volunteer at the Shalom Youth Centre, I did my best to work with young people in the way that the staff had worked with me. I made mistakes, I got things wrong, but I was trained to reflect on my mistakes, move on and do things differently in future.

"I wanted to better myself educationally but all that missed schooling had left me lacking in confidence and doubting my ability to cope. Once again John and the staff encouraged me and sent me on Youth work courses."

Michaela then moved on to explain all the projects she has been involved with at Shalom.

Grimsby has a major problem with what are classified as "Neets" – Not in education, employment or training. In fact it is one of the worst in the UK. One of the areas contributing to this problem are those children who are excluded from school. It means that apart from all the other difficulties they experience, this group does not have access to the services available to bridge the transition from school to further education or employment.

"We started the Space project, an exclusion unit. Obviously our target group, excluded kids were very challenging but as long as you establish a relationship with them and show that you are someone who bothers about them, you have the base to build on. Everyone has an interest or a talent, it's about identifying it and nurturing it. Franklin College were excellent and gave us good support in Literacy and Numeracy and the Connexions Service came in from Leeds to give careers and further education advice. We introduced Health & Safety courses, Sea Survival and CS cards to enable them to work on factory shutdowns or on the offshore oil rigs. Other courses included CV compilation, interview techniques and courses on mental health. We worked on the Duke of Edinburgh Award Scheme and in three years had over 200 on our books."

I asked Michaela to talk about some of the problems and successes of the Space Project.

"About a quarter were always up against it. They were poorly dressed, erratic timekeepers and often had problems with drink or drugs. Chaotic home backgrounds did not provide the vital stability they needed to turn things around."

The successes are many. Indeed, I was given a copy of, of all things the Sunday Mail magazine of 21st October 2007. This outlined in great detail some amazing personal stories. The most spectacular is that of Thomas Turgoose, the award-winning young star of the gritty film, "This is England", whose talent was spotted when he was 13, after the film's Casting Director came looking for unknowns with acting potential. Tommo, as he is known, has never forgotten his roots and his charity work has seen the Shalom as a major beneficiary.

Also in the article, Arron Bradley's story is no less inspirational. Excluded from school and a virtual outcast, his love of motorbikes was utilised and with support used to give him a career as a motor mechanic.

Michaela then moved to running the Shalom Youth Project. On Thursday nights, 12 – 14 years olds are catered for and on Fridays, 14 upwards.

"You can see some kids who start with real disadvantages. Things like a good start to the day given at Havelock School with their breakfast policy makes all the difference. It's these simple basics that are so essential. Rather than the constant demonising of young people they should be a priority. We need to build their confidence and sense of self, they are the future of this community."

Finally I asked about the Soup Kitchen, open three days a week catering for about 50 people on an average day.

"It all started with a well-known homeless man who we found in our entrance. He was desperate and we fed him. More and more came, the hungry, the homeless, some with drink and drug issues and some driven to despair by the "sanctions" regime."

Michaela's workload and commitment is phenomenal. I asked her to summarise her own journey and her aspirations for the future.

"John, Jackie and the staff here have made me what I am today. I have passed on my experiences and what I have learned to my children and I am very proud of what they have become. John encouraged me to do a degree in Youth and Community work. I feel that I have a purpose in life. John and Jackie have got me where I am, I want to do this for others.

"As for my aspirations for Shalom, I would like to work with families, getting parents involved in tea-time groups. It would be nice if we could have more paid, full-time staff to supplement our dedicated volunteers. Finally, I would like to see major investment in this community and real jobs come out of it. To my mind, once the jobs disappeared this was the trigger for the issues we face today."

The Shalom's contribution to this community and to so many people in it cannot be measured. No Shalom over the last 40 years on the East Marsh is too chilling a prospect to contemplate.

"BRIDGE OVER TROUBLED WATER" – DAVE CARLISLE
(SIMON & GARFUNKEL)

23 WATKINS STREET

Dave is another example of a fascinating life story spanning the entire period of this book.

Unlike virtually everyone else, Dave was born and lived the early part of his life on the West Marsh – one side of the street's catchment area was Harold Street and so the dye was cast. He explained.

"There was an unwritten rule almost then, Dockers lived on the West Marsh and fishermen lived on the East Marsh. My Dad was a docker. My Mum worked as a butcher on Freeman Street market. My brother went to Loughborough University and is now a draughtsman in South Africa. My sister is a hairdresser.

"Looking back, it was a good time to grow up. There were loads of timber yards to play in. The demolition of some streets was in full swing and provided loads of opportunities to start fires and other bits of mayhem.

"We moved to a house on the Willows Estate but by this time I had started at Harold Street and had no intention of changing. I always think I had a good education there.

"I intended to go to Whitgift Sixth Form but at the last minute applied for two apprenticeships instead. There was a draughtsman's job at Fowler and Holdens, the engineers and also a motor mechanic's at Hartfords. When I arrived for interview, the motor mechanics job had already been taken but they offered me an HGV Fitter's position. I thought bird in hand and started immediately completing my apprenticeship in 1981. I decided to go self-employed and got a lock-up on the old Consolidated Fisheries Yard at Riby Square. I was in this for five years but was offered a job with a tyre company. I did a year in Grimsby and six years in Scunthorpe.

"I suffer from Behcet's Syndrome – it attacks your immune system – it has plagued me all my working life, although at the moment it is stable.

"Whilst on a lengthy period off work on the sick, I decided to do some GCSEs to get back into the rhythm of study. I picked maths, Physics, History and Sociology. I was 30 years of age in a class of 16-year olds. However, although it went well I still had no plan for my future.

"I decided to enrol on a two-year Diploma in Higher Education and got a small grant, how times change! I had got the bug and signed up for a BA in Humanities and this took a further year to top up from my Diploma.

"Then I got a real breakthrough. I was offered some teaching on the Refrigeration Course at Grimsby college. The group I inherited were miles behind on the projects they were doing. They were hacked off and very resentful. I managed to calm them down and we put a plan together. I said I'll get you through this. I gained a great deal of satisfaction from working with these students and guiding them to a successful outcome.

"Obviously I had an engineering background and more work was offered on GNVQ Engineering courses majoring on Business Studies and Environmental Studies. I enrolled on a two-year, part-time Teaching Diploma and used my classes to build up my observations and teaching practice.

"I then started doing work in the community which I really enjoyed. We went into schools to work with parents who wanted to return to education. We had a group at Welholme Junior School and started them on Local History and then moving on to Sociology and European Studies.

"However I was becoming increasingly disillusioned with Grimsby College. I knew that my vocation lay in community work and I became a Community Development Worker on the Yarborough and Nunsthorpe Estates.

"I then moved after eighteen months to my present job in 2004 as Project Co-ordinator for volunteers at Harbour Place."

I asked Dave to explain what harbour Place is all about. Dave explained.

"We work with people, primarily from the East Marsh to gain accommodation and give them the support to keep it. I write the funding bids and our main source of cash is the National Lottery. We have had three successful bids. We have six full-time and one part-time staff, as well as about fifteen volunteers. Our client group is 75% single homeless males primarily aged between 25 – 54 years of age. As well as running a Day Centre and providing meals we have just started a night shelter for rough sleepers although we can only accommodate about a dozen. The problem is just getting worse. This week we had eight with us on Monday night but we spoke to sixteen who were on the streets. Jimmy Hill, another ex-Harold Street lad is our permanent night worker. He is great and has the ability to talk to and get on with everyone.

"People become homeless for many reasons. Illness, unemployment, relationship breakdowns, drug and alcohol problems. Drugs especially on the East Marsh. Many have come through the care system and have had it tough right from the start. I will have been here 14 years this March. It is a fantastic job. Hull University approached us to give students placements as part of the practical element of their Social Work Degree. I became what is known as a Practice Educator to mentor and guide them – we have had 18 students in 14 years.

"When the rules changed, I could no longer fulfil this role without a Social Work Degree myself. So I thought needs must, and did a BSC in Social Work over four years. I am now on the Hull University Reading Panel to assess students' coursework."

This sums up Dave entirely. If an obstacle is put in front of him, he simply takes whatever steps are required to overcome it.

I then turned to ask Dave what is necessary to improve the situation on the East Marsh.

"I'll tell you what won't improve things. Universal Credit just means racking up debt whilst you're waiting for it. Personal Independence Payments are a disgrace – one client has been waiting eleven and a half months for a decision. The lack of social housing and the benefit cuts, The Bedroom Tax and the absolute shortage of one-bedroom properties all point to a bad problem simply worsening. The East Marsh has become a ghetto of multi-occupancy housing.

"We took some of our volunteers down to London. We visited a Day Centre in Westminster. It was breath-taking, like another world – millions had been spent on an upgrade. We have found similar examples in Glasgow and Liverpool. Big cities seem to be a magnet for whatever investment there is to go around.

"I think Freeman Street has seen a bit of a recovery with all the shops and businesses opened by Eastern Europeans and Turks. To really regenerate the area Grimsby Town Football Club should have relocated on the site of the multi storey flats with all the attendant new properties. That would have been a real shot in the arm."

Finally, Dave demonstrated his great attachment to the area. The other night I watched Grimsby town at the Warehouse and regularly have a pint down Freeman Street. "I enjoy it, I know loads of people and ironically there is never any trouble."

PART FOUR - "TRANSFORMATION"
(VAN MORRISON, 2017)

Tony Benn once said, "There is no final victory, as there is no final defeat. There is just the same battle to be fought, over and over again. So toughen up, bloody toughen up."

He went on, "From the beginning of time there have been two flames burning in the human heart. The flame of anger against injustice, and the flame of hope that you can build a better world."

Tony added that it was his job, "To go around fanning both flames."

The three periods in history covered by this book – the late sixties and early seventies; the period 1979 – 86 and finally the present day were all periods of Conservative government.

In this passage of time of almost fifty years there has been an inexorable movement rightwards and an increasingly harsh policy response to the seemingly intractable problems facing Britain.

Although as we have seen Heath was prevented from introducing much of his programme by massive working class pressure, Thatcher set about her task with ruthless determination. The balance of class forces was firmly tilted in favour of capital, and the doctrines of neo-liberalism dominated henceforth.

When Thatcher was asked what was her greatest achievement, she replied, "Tony Blair and New Labour".

She said, "We forced our opponents to change their minds."

The more New Labour became wedded to this economic regime, albeit with some of the rough edges taken off by increased public expenditure, the more alternatives were denounced.

New Labour and the Conservatives were now positioned on a tiny piece of right of centre turf with policies of broad similarity. Blair's Government accepted the Thatcherite totems of privatisation, deregulation of the city and the Private Finance Initiative. Blair never seemed happier than when attacking his own supporters, whether they were Trade Unionists or public sector workers.

The more Blair then Brown departed from and redefined the party's purpose, the more disillusioned people became with politics. Millions of voters left Labour as increasingly the tired maxim, "They're all the same" became a reality.

The election of Jeremy Corbyn as Labour leader marks a real fracturing of the neo-liberal consensus. His ideas and policies, most of which he has held all his political life, were a surprising revelation to younger voters. Many were exposed to ideas for the first time that had been ignored, suppressed or regarded with amused contempt by the Blairites.

Corbyn was prepared to oppose the Government's austerity programme and support higher public spending, nationalisation and redistribution. Hardly the stuff of which revolutions are made. His pledge to end austerity and instead implement a People's Quantative Easing Programme means that money would be invested in infrastructure, job creation and high technology industries. He also firmly addressed the housing crisis through an ambitious home-building programme to fully nationalise key industries such as rail and bring all academies back under local democratic control.

The politics represented by Corbyn were supposed to be finished, consigned to the dustbin of history. With virtually no alternative to capitalism voiced since 1989 it is indeed a massive breakthrough to read surveys showing British people to be slightly "Keener on socialism than on capitalism."

This sea change has come about for two main reasons. The crash of 2007 – 8 highlighted both an unbalanced economy and an unregulated financial sector brought down by its own g

Endless austerity, concentrated on those least able to cope

demonstrated beyond doubt the implausibility of Osborn

mantra, "We are all in this together." With real wages plummetin

and the constant pushing back of deficit reduction targets, the

system has been under scrutiny like never before with the onset of

economic stagnation and austerity without end.

Corbyn has exploited this opening caused by the increasing disenchantment with policy responses. He has produced a radical alternative to austerity. This alternative is not the "Too far too fast" version of Rachel Reeves and Ed Balls – austerity with a human face. It is not the reformism without reforms, espoused by too many Labour MPs. It is a genuine social democratic alternative that puts investment not cuts, at the heart of its programme.

As of writing this, Labour are ahead in the polls and the Tories are in turmoil. The Tory Party Conference of 2017 will go down in history as one of the worst since the war. However, it is not the coughing fits of the P45 stunt or the falling letters on the backdrop that are important. What was revealed was the absolute timidity and bankruptcy of the policy response to the serious problems facing society. The fact that "Right to Buy" has been resurrected once again shows that growth, any growth, is welcomed even if it is attained by stoking up yet another house price boom.

‎crossroads. What is required in towns like ‎ne elements of Corbyn's programme. Investment ‎stock, green technology, much of which is labour ‎o provide career opportunities, the restoration and ‎f the Welfare State, the NHS and Education.

‎n's programme offers hope, hope against a brutal neo-liberal ‎ology which has patently failed the mass of people in society. Many of those interviewed in this book expressed concerns about the future of their children and grandchildren. Concerned that even if they display the same amount of guts and graft they did, the diminished opportunities on offer mean a life of insecurity and worry.

The next election marks possibly the last chance to fundamentally change things for Grimsby and the East Marsh. It is not merely winning the election, it is about changing the course of history by a permanent transformation in the balance of power in favour of the many not the few. To transform a system currently rigged against working people.

There is a line in the famous film, "The Shawshank Redemption". Andy Dufresne (Tim Robbins) tells fellow convict Ellis Boyd "Red" Redding (Morgan Freeman) "Hope is a good thing maybe the best of things, and no good thing ever dies".

NOTES

<u>Preface</u>

Aditya Chackrabortty - "Why doesn't Britain make things anymore" Guardian, 16th November 2011

Peter Mandleson - "Developing UK Industrial Policy". ESAD, December 2009

Rachel Shabi - "Poll after poll shows that the party policies under the leadership of Jeremy Corbyn have popular support". Guardian, 30th September 2017

Boris Johnson - "My vision for a bold thriving Britain enabled by Brexit". Telegraph, 15th September 2017

<u>Part One 1970 – 1974</u>

James Callaghan – Labour Party Conference 1976

William Beveridge - Social Insurance and Allied Services – November 1942

John Maynard Keynes – The General Theory of Employment, Interest and Money – February 1936

Edward Heath – "On reducing prices at a stroke" – Tory proposals to revoke taxation – 1970

Jimmy Reid – "Reflections of a Clyde-Built Man" – 1976

ok – "State of Emergency: The Way We Were 1974" – 2011

eron – Conservative Party Conference, Manchester – 2nd r 2013

s Johnson – Conservative Party Conference, Manchester – 2nd October 2013

Jim Jackson – Measure of Domestic Progress (MDP), Jim Jackson and Nat McBride, University of Surrey – 11th July 2005

Part Two – The Rise of Thatcherism 1979 – 1986

Michael Deacon – "The Funeral of Margaret Thatcher – How applause drowned out the jeers" – Telegraph, 17th April 2013

Milton Friedman – "Capitalism and Freedom" – 1962

Friedrich Hayeck – "The Road to Serfdom" – 1944

Ian McGregor – "The Enemies Within – The Story of The Miners' Strike 1984 – 85" – Ian McGregor and Rooney Tyler – 1986

Dan Finn – "Training without Jobs – New Deals and Broken Promises" – 1987

Frederick Winslow Taylor – "Scientific Management" – 1909

Clive Morton – "Becoming World Class" – 1994

Larry Elliott/Dan Atkinson – "Lawson, Leahy and a Quarter Cen of Illusions" – "The Gods That Failed" – 2009

J. K. Galbraith – "The Affluent Society" – 1958

Harry Leslie Smith – "Don't Let My Past Be Your Future: A Call to Arms" – 2017

Part Four – Transformation

Tony Benn – "Every Generation Must Fight the Same Battles Again and Again" – speech 25th April 2012

Margaret Thatcher "Tony Blair and New Labour – we forced our opponents to change their minds" – attributed to an after-dinner speech for Conor Burns, later MP for Bournemouth West – 2002

The Shawshank Redemption – 1994

ury

Printed in Great Britain
by Amazon